DON'T GAMBLE WITH YOUR RETIREMENT

No-Risk Strategies for a Secure Future

ROZ KOVEL with SHON PEIL

EXPERT PRESS

DON'T GAMBLE WITH YOUR RETIREMENT
No-Risk Strategies for a Secure Future

Printed in the United States of America.

Shon Peil
Retirement Shield LLC
24 Roy St #432
Seattle, WA 98109
www.RetirementShield.us

Expert Press
www.ExpertPress.net

—Disclaimer—

The information provided in this book is for informational purposes only and is not intended to be a source of advice or credit analysis with respect to the material presented. The information and/or documents contained in this book do not constitute legal or financial advice and should never be used without first consulting with an insurance and/or a financial professional to determine what may be best for your individual needs.

The publisher and the author do not make any guarantee or other promise as to any results that may be obtained from using the content of this book. You should never make any investment decision without first consulting with your own financial advisor and conducting your own research and due diligence. To the maximum extent permitted by law, the publisher and the author disclaim any and all liability in the event any information, commentary, analysis, opinions, advice and/or recommendations contained in this book prove to be inaccurate, incomplete or unreliable, or result in any investment or other losses.

Although the author and publisher have made every effort to ensure that the information in this book was correct at press time, the author and publisher do not assume and hereby disclaim any liability to any party for any loss, damage, or disruption caused by errors or omissions, whether such errors or omissions result from negligence, accident, or any other cause.

Content contained or made available through this book is not intended to and does not constitute legal advice or investment advice and no attorney-client relationship is formed. The publisher and the author are providing this book and its contents on an "as is" basis. Your use of the information in this book is at your own risk.

Contents

Don't Gamble With YOUR Retirement

Walking Away From the Table

If you're a good gambler, you know that there comes a time when you should take some of your winnings off the table. Far too often, people stay at the table too long and lose everything.

I know what I'm talking about. I grew up with bad gamblers. My parents were gambling addicts. Almost every night they'd leave home at 10 p.m. and return at 4 a.m. the next morning, spending that time at a local (illegal) gambling casino. My father was such a high roller that some Las Vegas casinos paid to fly him there to shoot craps — many times! I remember one night in 1956 when my dad lost $150,000 (almost $1.5 million in today's dollars) within a couple of hours.

Their addiction was extreme and it cost me the education I had dreamed of. Before my freshman year of college, when money was good, my parents told me I could go to any school I wanted. But when good money turned bad within a year, they told me I would have to drop out. Unpredictable was what life was like being tied to the gaming tables.

My parents gambled away a multimillion-dollar fortune they earned in the textile industry, causing our family to live in a constant state of financial uncertainty. No amount of good business sense could have saved them from themselves.

You may be saying that you're nothing like my parents. You don't gamble, and if you do, you're sensible. But I'm here to tell you that leaving most of your money in the market is no different from continuing to ride a lucky streak in blackjack. You're jeopardizing your future and your family's well-being by trying to make a little more or turning your luck around. Why put so much on the line when there are better, safer ways to make enough to retire?

Before the financial crash of 2008 hit, I thought I was in a good financial position. I was working for a software company that helped people cancel their debt. I was doing quite well and my investment portfolio was strong, or so I thought. I was even toying with the idea of retiring within the next five years.

Then, almost overnight, everything changed. The software company went under and my job disappeared. I lost half the equity in my home and half the value of my "smart" investments. The person I trusted to invest my money had left me 100% exposed to the market. All of my money was in stocks, bonds, and mutual funds. And now, more than half of it was gone.

For the second time in a decade, I found myself losing half of my money. And now, I was much closer to retirement.

I vowed that I would never let this happen to me again, and if I could, I'd make sure it didn't happen to anyone else either.

Taking My Finances Into My Own Hands

Instead of shrugging my shoulders at this loss as I had after the 2002 crash, I realized I had been abdicating my responsibility for my own financial education and decisions, leaving my financial well-being totally in the hands of my advisor. I was devastated but felt defiant. I just needed a way forward, and then, one arrived in the mail. It was an advertisement for a seminar — similar to the seminars I do now — that said I could learn how to protect my money to avoid another 2008. I signed up right away.

That seminar changed my life. I didn't even know there were investment vehicles that could guarantee I would never lose money again. I wasn't aware there were financial tools that could provide income for life. I didn't know there were smarter ways to approach my finances, then, today, and in retirement. All of my knowledge up to that point had come from my financial advisor and the media, and it turned out I was only getting part of the story.

As far as most financial professionals are concerned, your only option to protect yourself is a "diversified portfolio of stocks, bonds, and mutual funds" that keeps all your money in the market. That's an excellent option when you're young, and it's fine for part of your money as you get older. But it doesn't help you avoid another "worst-case" scenario that could come without warning (like what happened in 2002, 2008, and most recently, in 2020). For that, you need a completely different set of strategies.

Helping Those Who Don't Know What They Don't Know

As soon as I learned about these new strategies, I decided I wanted to share what I'd learned with others. I wanted to help everyone avoid what I'd gone through … twice!

Far too often I meet people who are in the same position I was before the last crash: They don't even know there's another way to grow their money.

That was certainly the case with James, a man who attended my very first Retirement Shield seminar. I can't say he was completely unaware of his risks. He knew there was something wrong with his investment strategies; he just didn't know what the solution was.

As it turned out, James was an accountant who was extremely knowledgeable about finance. He was well-educated on the subject and had numerous initials trailing his name to indicate his various degrees and certifications. James even taught finance classes for graduate students part-time at one of the local colleges.

But James had a blind spot in all his financial knowledge. There was no greater expert on corporate finance in Illinois than James, but he had begun to realize that he was not as astute about his personal financial picture. That's what brought him to me.

James was approaching retirement age and he knew he had run out of time to get these strategies right. He wanted to retire early from a job that he didn't enjoy, but he needed help with organizing his finances so that could happen.

"How much do you have set aside for retirement?" I asked him.

It was over $1 million, but James didn't feel those investments were secure enough for him to leave his job.

So I walked him through many of the ideas in this book and showed him how he could protect his income enough to retire at the end of the year.

"How much of my savings should I invest?" he asked.

I told him $300,000, but James was smart enough to know I was lowballing.

"I know that you recommended what you thought I would agree to. How much do you think I should *really* move?"

"Six hundred thousand dollars," I told him.

James did more than that. He transferred over $600,000 into products I recommended for him. And as a result, he's been able to retire early and with complete security.

Carole was in a similar situation. Unlike James, she liked her job. But to work the full-time first shift she had to get up at 4 a.m., five days a week, and it was making her miserable. As a 62-year-old widow with grandchildren, Carole was ready to step back and enjoy her time with her family.

Unfortunately, she'd gotten some bad advice about Social Security. She was told that she couldn't get widow's benefits until she reached full retirement age at 66 ½. She'd have to work almost five more years before she could retire. When she heard this, Carole burst into tears.

But she didn't give up. She dried her eyes and came to me. I told her that she not only *did* qualify for her widow's benefit immediately but I also told her how to get it. This put her in a position to bargain with her employer. Her boss immediately agreed to her request for a part-time position on second shift, allowing her to sleep later and spend time with her grandkids.

Instead of waiting half a decade for the life she wanted, Carole had it within weeks. But she could only achieve that life because she realized that she didn't have all the answers to her financial situation. Carole needed help and got it. Her grandchildren are as grateful for that as she is.

It's Not Just Money; It's Your Time

Retirement is about more than just the dollars in your account; it's also about time. James and Carole wanted more time for themselves and their families. They wanted to spend less time working in unsatisfactory conditions and more time enjoying their retirement.

Time is always a concern when it comes to retirement, and not just because you want more years of freedom, family, and fun. The timing of your retirement makes a significant difference in your financial health. In retirement planning, we often talk about a concept called sequence of returns risk. The sequence of returns shows it isn't just about how much you have invested, but it's how those investments fare early on in your retirement. If you retire into a strong market, you can build up enough wealth to see you through decades of retirement. But if you experience losses, even a sizable retirement account can dry up within a few years … unless you do something to protect your money beforehand.

Unfortunately, we could be looking at an extremely negative market over the next few years. If you make the wrong choices today, you may leave yourself with undesirable options: Work well into your retirement years or try to manage on far less than you expected.

That's why, if you want to shield yourself from the worst-case retirement scenarios, the time to start exploring your options is now.

If Your Ideas Are So Good, Why Isn't Everyone Talking About Them?

When I explain all this to my clients, they often ask me the same question: "Why haven't I heard any of this before?"

Clients like James have been in the financial industry for decades, yet they either don't know or have heard negative opinions about the strategies I recommend.

It isn't because the ideas are bad. Nor is it because they're new or radical. It's simply that the majority of investment advisors ignore these strategies because they aren't within the array of products these advisors are trained and licensed to recommend.

I've been getting the AARP magazine for years, and they often advise getting your finances in order in preparation for retirement. Yet every time I open the pages expecting to see Retirement Shield ideas, I end up disappointed; there's never a word about the strategies we use.

Even many of the big financial gurus out there refuse to acknowledge these ideas. They tell you to invest more and smarter in the market alone in a "diversified portfolio of stocks, bonds, and mutual funds." That's their only advice and that's a good idea. I encourage market investments, but in addition, there are *guaranteed* ways to protect your money, particularly as you enter retirement.

The problem is there's a cold war going on between market investors and those who offer alternative, safer investment options. It doesn't need to be a point of conflict, but far too often, traditional advisors feel that endorsing these ideas costs them business.

Your financial picture shouldn't be an either-or situation; it should be a both-and situation. You can invest in the market *and* still put aside enough to protect yourself no matter what happens.

That's one of the reasons I wanted to be involved in this book. The people you have listened to may be keeping some of these ideas from you. And it's time to get the word out.

I've Faced It All So You Don't Have To

I overcame a lot in my life: destructive parents, poor investments, even the loss of my husband at an early age. My mission is to make sure you don't have to face so many challenges as you head into retirement.

Throughout life I've gained strength from my family — my children, my grandchildren, and my dogs. It was a dog, a collie named Baron, who helped me through my difficult childhood. Now my dogs have helped me provide some companionship for seniors in retirement homes. I make sure all my dogs are certified therapy dogs so they can go and spread a little joy to those who can really use it.

So I know how important family can be, and I also understand the strain finances can put on that family.

When you gamble with too much of your money in the market during retirement, or you don't prepare for risks like long-term care — a need 70% of us will have at some point in our lives — you expose not just yourself to risk, but everyone you love.

That's something you just don't have to do. And to avoid that future is painless. I make sure that an appointment with me is as easy, comfortable, and beneficial as possible. When we first meet, I make sure the first thing you feel is at home. At our initial appointment, I ask you to share your ideal retirement future. I explain my process, and you ask all of your questions. We then slowly work our way through the strategies that may work best for you. My passion is teaching, so I make sure my clients understand all the details about the programs they're considering so they can make an informed decision.

Avoiding traumatic financial insecurity is as simple as setting up an appointment.

The Power of a Retirement Shield

Before I entered the financial coaching world, I worked in preventative health care, helping people avoid future health problems by guiding them to better lifestyle choices: a focus on nutrition, exercise, and stress management.

Honestly, I don't think I ever really changed professions. Now I just look at a different side of wellness. Getting your financial wellness in order is as critical to a good retirement as your health.

But financial wellness requires a comprehensive approach, just as medicine does. One of my mentors in the retirement planning industry says that you should not work with a planner who doesn't present four key solutions: Social Security, annuities, life insurance, and long-term care. Unfortunately, plenty of companies do not address all of these topics; I know because I've had to leave such companies in the past.

That's what attracted me to Shon and Retirement Shield. Unlike so many in this industry, Retirement Shield provides a full picture of your retirement options.

And that's why I'm so proud to be a part of this book. Shon has been a wonderful coach to me, and it's been a joy seeing how our values align in this book.

In these pages you'll find information about all the moving parts you have to account for to have the retirement of your dreams. People's two greatest retirement fears are losing their money and running out of money, and this book will provide you with the peace of mind you need to put those fears to rest for good.

The ideas in these pages are critical to anyone ready to walk away from the retirement gambling table and concentrate on putting their financial health first. You need these ideas, whether you're a financial wiz like James, a financial novice like Carole, or anyone in between. You need comprehensive assistance to explore all your options so that you aren't left with too much risk or spending too much time making up for losses you didn't have to suffer.

That's what the Retirement Shield program offers. And that's what I aim to provide every client.

Chapter 1

Based on a True Story

From Wheelchair to Walking

I was 24 years old, and I literally could not move. I was in the worst pain of my life.

My wife Hillary was in school, and I was the sole provider for our family. We were newly married, and Hillary was determined to help me. We were desperate; I hadn't walked for almost 18 months, and I was losing hope. She called a friend who worked downtown in a back specialist's office and asked them to take a look at my chart in the hopes that they could find an answer.

No more than 20 minutes later, the office called, and the nurse told her, "You need to get Shon down here right away." She loaded me into the car — meaning that she put me in the back of the car where you'd put your dogs — and I kind of sprawled out while she drove us down to the hospital.

At the hospital, the doctor told me, "We're going to do an MRI." I had already been through so many MRIs and was tired of being poked and prodded, but the doctor was adamant that another test was necessary. I was extremely overweight, depressed, and in tremendous pain. Moving me into the machine only magnified that pain. Once inside the metal tube, I shifted and sobbed because the pain was so intense.

The nurse said, "Shon, if you can just stay still, you're going to be all right. We'll get done quickly." She kept to her word, and before I knew it, she was wheeling me into the doctor's well-appointed office. I had seen numerous specialists and had come away feeling hopeless — but something this time felt different.

When the surgeon came into the room, he saw that I had moved from the wheelchair to the floor in an effort to relieve a fraction of my pain. He showed me two images — one of a healthy spine and the other an MRI of my spine — and said, "Shon, this is what your spine is supposed to look like, but L4 and L5 have exploded and are lodged within your tailbone."

I was in shock. I couldn't even speak. Did this mean there was hope, or was my condition irreversible? The surgeon recognized the terror in my eyes, and he quickly assured me that he could correct the problem, and I could lead a normal life again. He told me, "You need surgery, and you need it now." We didn't hesitate. My wife signed the paperwork, and the nurse whisked me away to prepare me. I was on the operating table just hours later.

Miraculously, when I awoke, my pain was completely gone. The absence of pain was foreign to me; I didn't know how to react. I felt like myself again, but I worried that it was only temporary. Could I dare to hope this was the end of my long nightmare?

My medical team didn't waste any time. I was up and walking by the end of that same evening. And over the next few days, I threw everything I had into my physical therapy.

I was discharged shortly after surgery and haven't looked back since.

Unseen Black Ice

That day changed my life. I often wonder what would have happened if my wife hadn't taken a proactive approach and if we hadn't sought that second opinion. Where would I be today?

The surgery marked the end of almost two years of misery that started with a car accident. I had been on a business trip when the car I was riding in hit some black ice and ran head-on into an embankment. At the time, I didn't think there was much wrong, just that my knee hurt a bit. But over the next couple of weeks, it became apparent that my knee wasn't the problem. My back began to hurt, and it got worse and worse. I tried everything — from chiropractic to acupuncture to physical therapy. You name it, I tried it, but nothing helped. The pain kept intensifying until I could no longer walk.

At one point, I saw a doctor who gave me a cortisone shot to try to take away the pain. Unfortunately, when they gave me the shot, they missed and numbed everything below my waist. After that, I was extremely gun shy and fearful of getting another opinion, but that second opinion and the resulting surgery changed my life. My wife and I now have five beautiful little kids — 10-year-old twins, an eight-year-old, a three-year-old, and a newborn.

An Unclear Future

During those long months of suffering, so many things went through my mind. I kept wondering: *What is this going to look like? Are we going to have kids? Am I ever going to get back to the sports and active lifestyle that I've always loved?* Fear of the unknown caused many sleepless nights.

Today, when I work with clients, I remember how I lived in that fear of the unknown. It parallels what I see in the people I meet who fear the unknown concerning their retirement. For twenty-some years of my life, I was incredibly active, and then it suddenly ended. For many people, retirement hits almost as abruptly.

When people begin to think about retirement, they don't know what to expect. Clients often say, "Oh, I'll never fully retire," which I often believe is because they don't know what they're going to do with their time or how they are going to live when their life changes so dramatically. Fear of the unknown can be paralyzing, and it can prevent people from making plans.

After my life-changing injury, I didn't know how I was supposed to keep going when everything was so different from the life I once knew. I saw so many different doctors, and they all thought they had the answer — always a simple fix. But it's often more complicated than it seems, and, usually, it's not just one issue that needs addressing. For me, it was a couple of different things that made everything work. The same is true for folks contemplating retirement. It's a multi-pronged approach.

A Solid Plan

When people start thinking about retirement, they're trying to envision what it's supposed to look like. Most people have been receiving a consistent paycheck, many with some kind of benefits and vacation time. Throughout their 30 to 40 working years, every decision about these kinds of things has almost always been made for them, but now they have to rely on themselves to make some of these decisions. With that comes many questions:

- How do I replace income when I'm no longer getting a paycheck?
- How do I make sure I have enough money to live on?
- How do I make sure I have enough money to address any medical concerns?

Usually, throughout a person's working career, they save up for different family events, vacations, or major purchases. But if they're not going to be accumulating any more money, where does the money come from when they need a newer car, a home repair, or something else? They begin to wonder how it's all going to work when the paychecks stop and start asking themselves if they will have enough money to accomplish your goals after retirement.

Yes, there are a lot of question marks. I always tell my clients, "You wouldn't build a house without a plan, and you can't expect to build your retirement without a plan." Unfortunately, most people — I'd estimate 95% of all Americans — whether they are retired or going to retire, don't have a plan in place. They don't have a concrete or comprehensive strategy for addressing what will happen in the next 15 or 20 years.

People need to ask themselves what they want from their retirement years. Naturally, those answers will be different for everyone, but there are some common themes. People want their retirement to be free of stress. They want freedom and security.

So how are you going to achieve those things? How are you going to achieve freedom from stress unless you put together a plan to alleviate the different strains of retirement? For example, if your goal is to maximize your Social Security, how are you going to do that unless you've consulted with an expert and proactively gone through the numbers to make sure you're getting the best benefit for you and your family?

How are you going to ensure that you don't pay more in taxes? You're going to do that by putting a tax plan in place as soon as possible.

How are you going to protect yourself from market volatility? The market has been robust, but it will go down. That's not a matter of if but a matter of when. The market goes up, and it goes down. What are you doing now that you weren't doing maybe four, five, or even 10 years ago, so that when volatility hits, you get different results? What are you doing to make sure you're not hurt as you might have been in previous market declines?

Being Proactive

We've helped our clients answer these questions through proactive planning. Having a plan in place has helped our clients address all these different areas, allowing them to adjust as life happens.

That's what it's all about. Life happens, and you can't know what the future holds, but you can put a plan in place to be ready for whatever the future may bring.

The sooner you have a strategy for each of these areas, the better off you're going to be, and the better you will sleep at night. Having a plan will put to rest a lot of the anxiety that comes with the word retirement.

We designed the Retirement Shield process to help you find answers to these questions and get concrete answers that provide you with security and peace of mind.

That's what makes the Retirement Shield process different. It's a comprehensive approach that looks at each aspect of planning and puts them together like the pieces of a puzzle to make a beautiful picture-perfect retirement for you while shielding against life's unknowns.

Our goals can only be reached through a vehicle of a plan, in which we must fervently believe and upon which we must vigorously act. There is no other route to success.

~ *Pablo Picasso*

Chapter 2

Why a Retirement Shield?

When my car hit that patch of black ice, I lost all control. I was at the mercy of outside forces and soon found myself dealing with the devastating consequences that resulted. Today, I talk with numerous people every month who are heading toward their patch of black ice in terms of their retirement.

Though they have saved all of their working careers, the outside forces of higher taxes, lower market returns, rising inflation, and the complexities of Social Security are preparing to wreak havoc on their hard-earned money. Some have taken a few precautions. Many others have no idea how to navigate these perils.

The Retirement Shield was inspired by my own experience of being proactive in making my recovery possible. If I had known there was black ice on the road ahead, I could have made some different decisions. The same is true for retirement planning.

The road to retirement may be filled with dips, curves, and some hidden black ice. If you have a good advisor, you may be able to navigate retirement safely. The problem is that many advisors aren't providing sound advice. For example, some of my clients are hearing "Wait it out," "The market will recover," "Don't look at your account balances," or "It's just a paper loss." This type of advice can create a wedge between a client and an advisor.

When my business partner and I created the Retirement Shield, we did it to fill a need we saw in the marketplace. We looked around and realized that our industry was lacking in what we considered to be real customer service.

In our experience, we've seen that the one thing people tend to know the least about is the one thing they have worked their whole life for — their money. It's also the one thing they're going to need the most throughout retirement and in any stage of life, and yet most people don't know much about making their money WORK to reach their goals and fulfill their dreams.

Education and Empowerment

Many of my industry colleagues don't want to deal with the educational piece of working with clients. It's time-consuming, and it's not lucrative. Most find it easier to refer clients to other specialists, such as the Social Security office or a tax professional.

That approach doesn't make sense. So, my business partner and I decided to create a process to educate people and empower them by talking about the things no one else does. We want our clients to be informed. It's so gratifying when a client says, "No one's ever told me that before," or "I've always wondered that, and I asked my guy this question, and he just said, 'Don't worry about it.'" These comments illustrate why we created the Retirement Shield process.

There is a better way to plan for retirement. Too many gaps occur when experts neglect to add value, simply because they don't want to deal with the resulting workload. Uncovering some of the issues clients have creates more work, but we're not afraid of that work. We want a long-lasting relationship with our clients, and we always want to add value. Ultimately, we identified specific areas of value that weren't currently being offered to clients by their advisors, and we addressed those issues with the Retirement Shield.

Designing Your Shield

The Retirement Shield is a comprehensive process that allows a client to be proactive in their approach to retirement planning. We designed it to help the client to get ahead of the four or five major areas that they need to get right in retirement.

The holistic nature of the Retirement Shield makes it unique in our industry. We're not just talking about Social Security or market volatility. Nor do we focus only on taxes or fees. This process addresses every aspect of retirement and ensures that they all work together. Our goal is to protect our clients' retirements from the things that can damage or destroy it.

A soldier going into battle or anyone confronting some kind of danger carries a shield for protection. Likewise, when you go into your retirement, you need protection against whatever may come. That's why we called our process the Retirement Shield.

We believe that, eventually, taxes will go up, and the market will experience some sort of volatility. We understand that people will always be sensitive to the fees they're paying and how that works. And we realize that Social Security is a huge issue. Some studies say that only 4% of Americans take Social Security at an optimal time to maximize their return.

The Social Security program is short on money, and there's going to be a shortfall. That means it's incredibly important to be making these decisions based on the most up-to-date guidelines about the way we can take Social Security. Winging it on any of these issues is not an option. Retirement Shield allows you to put all the pieces in place now so that when these things come up, you're protected.

A Complete Security Plan

All too often, when you are working with people in our industry, you get only a piece of the puzzle or a few of your questions answered. Retirement Shield is a comprehensive process that can stand alone because it addresses all of your questions and uniquely positions you in each one of the categories we're discussing, eliminating the need to go through multiple processes or consult with various specialists.

Most people I meet have many specialists addressing their retirement plan — including a financial advisor, a CPA, someone else discussing Social Security, and, perhaps, even another person helping with long-term care. My response is always, "Wait a minute. You really have to call four or five different people to get your answer?" That's ridiculous.

Since all of these issues impact your entire financial picture, you need to address them in a single plan that is easy to understand. After all, these things are related; a change in one area will most often affect another area. Doesn't it make more sense to address them together as part of a complete picture?

The goal of this process is to protect and grow you¬r nest egg. We want to maximize your income so that there's no shortage of money down the road. That includes mitigating and minimizing taxation so that it's not eating into your retirement income.

Since we developed the Retirement Shield, I have been talking in person and giving group presentations to people who are thinking about these issues and asking these questions.

In my 45-minute presentation, I lay the groundwork for the Retirement Shield process and present my "freedom-first" view of retirement so that people understand they have options. My goal is to alleviate the fears and misperceptions that are so common among people approaching retirement and to illustrate how having a plan in place allows them to replace their fear and anxiety with security and confidence.

I understand that timing is everything, and there's only so much information you can absorb from a packed 45-minute presentation. That's one of the reasons I decided to write this book — so that people can go at their own pace, have the information and subjects that they need to think about at their fingertips, and understand the questions that they need to be asking to put their Retirement Shield in place.

People process information in different ways, with some needing to hear something several times or read something several times for the material to sink in. Other people need to read and take notes or just have time to review and absorb the content slowly. Not everyone gets an opportunity to come to a class. Their work hours may make it impossible, or they may have health issues that prevent them from attending in person. As I have said before, life happens.

So with this book, I hope not only to build on my presentations but also to reach out to people who might not be able to attend a class or those who need more time to think about these questions. I believe strongly in this process, so I want to maximize its impact and share it as widely as possible.

The Retirement Shield process is taught by insurance and financial professionals all over the country to help their clients plan for and protect their retirement savings. One reason it works for so many people is that it's not a cookie-cutter approach.

Likewise, this is not a cookie-cutter book. There's no financial speak or industry speak or big-bank theology. It's not the 100-year-old rhetoric that we've been taught to believe about retirement. It is what's happening now.

Life has changed. The market has changed. The political landscape of America has changed. All of those things mean that retirement planning also has to change, just to catch up. I always tell my audiences that this is not your grandfather's retirement. The world is a different place, and we need to address that head-on.

Tom and Susan's "Black Ice"

It's one thing for me to say that this is not your grandpa's retirement and that you need to have a plan in place, but let's look at a real-life example:

Tom and Susan were planning to retire back in 2010, but they were hit squarely by the credit crisis and market correction of 2008.

Tom had worked for 25 years in a blue-collar position. He had excellent benefits but no pension, and almost everything that he was going to use for his retirement was in his 401(k) and Social Security. In the 2008 crash, Tom lost nearly 50 percent of his 401(k), and suddenly retirement was no longer an option. He had to spend the next 10 years continuing to work and contributing to his 401(k), relying on market growth to try to build it back up.

Having been burned so badly by the correction of 2008, Tom didn't have much faith in the market, so he missed out on a lot of the growth that has taken place in the past 10 years. His reaction was a common one; many people got out of the market and were understandably scared to get back in because they couldn't afford to go through it again — but that means they haven't appreciated all the growth that has happened since.

Tom's wife Susan was in the same boat. She didn't have as much in her 401(k), but now that money is going to be a more significant piece in the overall picture of their retirement income. It also meant that Susan had to continue working and contributing to her 401(k) so that at some point, they could both retire.

Tom finally retired in 2018, and Susan retired a year later. They both had to wait until age 70 to begin taking their

Social Security, and there's a good possibility that Tom might still need to work part time in retirement, as a result of the huge loss of 2008.

That's the big thing to remember. People like Tom and Susan without pensions have had to rely on their 401(k), a nest egg, or a savings account to take the place of a pension. When you suddenly lose 40 or 50 percent of that amount, your retirement prospects change quickly.

If Tom and Susan had a plan to take care of these possibilities, they would have been able to retire on schedule, but because there wasn't one in place, they had to work nearly 10 years longer than they intended. Unfortunately, most of us know folks who have experienced similar situations. No one wants to go through that.

Most people are going to remember the major market corrections of the past. The whole point of the Retirement Shield process is asking this question with our clients: **What have you done with your earnings and retirement money since then to make sure that never happens again?**

The last major correction was in 2008. That is until we were once again caught by surprise on February 20, 2020 (easy to remember by the date 02-20-20). Though it's is the first major correction of this decade, it's most likely not the last.

Time isn't on our side anymore. Gone is the time and the opportunity to rebuild accounts that have lost so much in value. Those are real dollars that are lost for good.

Let's take a closer look at just how the Retirement Shield process has helped our clients make that happen and how it could potentially protect yours too.

Good fortune is what happens when opportunity meets with planning.

~ Thomas Edison

Chapter 3

Social Security Shield

Social Security is critically important for most retirees, but many Americans know very little about its complexities. And because Social Security is so important, what you don't know about it can hurt you in your retirement.

A Solid Foundation

Social Security makes up a significant portion of baseline retirement income for most Americans. This figure is crucial because Americans in general — and Baby Boomers in particular — depend on it to create safety in retirement. What makes Social Security unique is that people work 30 or 40 years of their lives accumulating what they believe to be their Social Security benefits, then when it comes time to claim them, they get no direction on how best to do so.

Most people don't realize that there are options to choose from and many factors that should be considered when claiming their Social Security. These factors will help determine when you take it, how you take it, and how to maximize your benefit when you do. You've worked your whole life to accumulate the money that you've paid into Social Security, and as we always ask in our workshops, whose money is it?

It's your money, but the representatives at the Social Security office are specifically instructed not to provide advice when it comes to helping you navigate your claiming decision. So you better be well informed when it comes time to make your decision.

Social Security is also unique because it's a moving target. What that means is that Congress can make changes to the Social Security program at any time. For example, a couple of years ago, they phased out the two most valuable options, which were "file and suspend" and "restricted application." Most people said, "But they can't do that."

The truth, however, is that they did do that, and they can do it again. Social Security is running out of money. There's going to be a shortfall (currently projected to be somewhere around the year 2034 if nothing changes). So if they don't start making some changes to Social Security or limiting the ways you can take the benefit, the program may eventually run out of money, and the money that you paid in won't be there.

For instance, a working person in their late 40s won't claim Social Security for more than twenty-some years. They pay into the system every month, but when the time comes for them to begin taking their Social Security, their money most likely will not be there. Can that change? Yes, of course. It has been modified in the recent past and is likely to happen again (which is one of the challenges with Social Security — the rules continue to evolve). You have to remember this is about claiming your money. These are your hard-earned dollars, even though you didn't have a say about those dollars being put into the system.

The Ticking Time Bomb

The government established the Social Security system so that you put money in today, and you get it back someday in your retirement. The problem is most people don't get the full benefit of their Social Security. According to a study published in 2019, only 4% percent of Americans begin taking Social Security at the most optimal time. That means that the rest — the other 96% of retirees — are missing out on collecting a large portion of the money to which they are entitled. According to the same study, those retirees are losing out on a collective $3.4 trillion in retirement benefits (or more than $110,000 per household). So the government takes money out of each paycheck to make you pay into the system, but it doesn't teach you how to maximize your return when it's time to take your benefits. Who's really benefiting?

All of this makes Social Security a sort of ticking time bomb. If you don't get this right, it can make or break your retirement. Most people think, "Oh, I'm going to retire early and claim at 62," or "I'm going to retire and claim it at my full retirement age." They're just guessing and hoping for the best. That's not a plan for maximizing your Social Security.

We did a radio show for five years where we talked about retirement planning and took calls from listeners. The group of people who called most consistently were widows. The first thing every widow was trying to figure out was how to replace lost income. They would say, "He died too soon. He took care of this stuff. How much of his pension am I going to get?" (The harsh reality was that, usually, a spouse dying meant a 30 - 50% loss of household income.)

Typically, the widows thought the first thing they needed to do — if they hadn't already done so — was to rely on

Social Security. And almost every time, that wasn't the best option. There were other ways to stabilize their income that they were not aware of. This is incredibly important to understand; once you opt into Social Security and start taking your benefits, you can't go back and make changes. That's the challenge: Not only do you have to get it right, but you have to get it right the first time.

Have you ever wondered why this program is going broke? Consider this example: If someone were married for at least 10 years to three different spouses, each one of those spouses could potentially claim 50% of your benefits. You don't have to be a math major to understand that's 50% more than what you put in. If the government is consistently giving away more money than they have collected, it's no wonder that the program is going broke.

From Zero to a Million

Maria and Miguel immigrated to the United States 30 years ago. They raised their family while they both worked blue-collar jobs at a major California university their entire lives. Maria had stopped working two years before we met with them, and Miguel was planning on working for many more years to cover their expenses.

During our first meeting, they said, "We have no money saved and don't know what to do." It was heartbreaking to hear the situation this family found themselves in. Because they came from another country without a retirement system like the United States, and they were unaware of how the system worked, Maria and Miguel were unknowingly in a much better situation than they realized.

> After talking with them about their life and listening to their story, it became apparent that Maria and Miguel were confused about how Social Security and their pension fund could provide for them. They thought they were broke — but in reality, they had over $1 million available to them through their pension plans, plus the Social Security benefits they were entitled to. With a few phone calls to the university and some research on our end, we created a Retirement Shield for this couple using a proper combination of Social Security, pension, and long-term care coverage. With their shield in place, they are enjoying life beyond their wildest dreams.
>
> Matt S.
>
> Retirement Shield Coach in California

Many people are confused when it comes to Social Security, pension plans, and rollovers. That's why we take the time to understand your situation, explain in ordinary language how these work, and create a Retirement Shield plan that's right for you. We believe in building long-term relationships with our clients, which is why we prefer to earn your trust by doing the research up front, preparing a plan, and gaining your feedback before you ever decide to move forward.

By the way, Maria and Miguel took their first vacation to Hawaii recently, and he's choosing to retire in just a few months. Neither of them ever thought those events would happen.

If you're like Maria and Miguel and have questions about Social Security, income in retirement, or when you can stop working, talk with your Retirement Shield coach, and soon you could be living a life beyond your dreams as well.

When Should You Begin?

So when is the right time for you to start collecting Social Security?

In reality, this is a loaded question because there is no one "right" answer. The answer is different for each individual and each family. First of all, there are three main options when it comes to when you should begin collecting Social Security. You can:

- Start collecting before your full retirement age
- Start collecting at your full retirement age
- Start collecting after your full retirement age

Year of Birth*	Full Retirement Age
1943-1954	66
1955	66 and 2 months
1956	66 and 4 months
1957	66 and 6 months
1958	66 and 8 months
1959	66 and 10 months
1960 or later	67

* If you were born on January 1, use the prior year for "year of birth."

Let's look at each of those options.

Historically, the full retirement age was 65, but that has gradually increased, and if you were born in 1960 or later, your full retirement age is now 67. Regardless of your full retirement age, you can begin collecting Social Security as early as age 62. If you choose to collect early, however, your monthly benefit will be considerably less and result in a benefit reduction of as much as 30%.

You also need to consider that once you initiate Social Security and begin taking your benefit, that monthly check is not going to go up by 30% someday. You've locked in your monthly benefit amount for the rest of your life, with a few exceptions. So while we always look at that option, it very rarely makes sense to start taking Social Security early, unless your financial situation leaves you no other options.

The second option is to start collecting Social Security at your full retirement age, which will allow you to collect 100% of your benefits. For people who have worked 30 or 40 years, it's a nice amount of money and can work out really well. Though this is the option some people choose, you don't have to take your benefit at full retirement age, and delaying can offer some big advantages.

The third major option is delaying Social Security until after your full retirement age. Why might you choose to do that? For one thing, depending on what other income you might have, taking Social Security can affect your tax situation. Another reason to consider waiting is that your eventual monthly benefit increases for every month you delay past your full retirement age until you reach age 70.

So if you're able to let your benefit grow and delay collecting until age 70, your monthly benefit will be considerably higher. From full retirement age until age 70, your benefit increases at 8% per year. If your full retirement age is 66, for example, that means you could gain up to 32% growth in your monthly benefit by waiting until you turn 70. That growth compounds monthly, not annually, so if you plan to wait until age 70, and then your circumstances change (due to health or other issues) and you decide you need to start collecting at age 68, you will still see some growth.

That's a huge advantage: Every month after full retirement age, your benefit goes up. It's one of the things we always talk about with retirees and prospective retirees. Which of these three options makes the most sense for you and your family? What we can tell you from teaching hundreds of retirement classes is that the answer is different for almost everyone. There is no cookie-cutter answer.

Here's the bottom line. When you are making these critical decisions about Social Security, don't lock yourself into a loss if you don't have to. Allow your money the opportunity to pay you back. If there are other ways you can bridge that income gap in retirement — and there usually are — then you should do that. Many of you reading this book won't have pensions, and the only guaranteed payment in retirement you will have is your Social Security check. That's why it's essential to make the correct decision about how to take it. Once you make that choice, there's generally no changing it, so it's vital to make the right decision.

Pros and Cons

Since this is such a crucial decision, we want to make sure that you maximize the amount of money you receive. When we work with clients, we always consider the pros and cons of collecting Social Security early compared to waiting a number of years. For instance, a lot of people think to themselves, "Well, if I turn it on at age 62, I'll get maybe $1,000 a month, and I could use that." But if you wait until your full retirement age, that could be $1,500 or $1,600 a month. Over 10 years, that difference can pay for a lot of travel or other things.

If you wait till age 70, the amount you get is almost double what you would have gotten at age 62. Most of us would love it if our nest egg doubled in the next seven to 10 years, and that's what you have the chance to do with your Social Security benefit. You have an excellent opportunity to grow that lifetime benefit by delaying when you begin taking Social Security, so there are several factors you should consider.

Longevity

One of those factors is longevity. How long are you likely to live? Is there a history of longevity in your family? On average, people are living longer than ever before. They also tend to underestimate how long they will live.

It's like the changes we have seen in technology. If someone had told you 10 years ago what we would be able to do now on a cell phone, you wouldn't have believed it. But look at the little minicomputers we carry around as phones today and consider the technological advancements that occurred in the last 10 years. In those same years, medicine has also made astounding progress, and over the next 10 to 15 years, people are likely to continue living even longer. Some of the diseases that we don't think are preventable or curable now will probably be preventable and curable by then.

What does all this mean? If people are living longer — and healthier — they're going to need more money. They're going to spend more money, and, as we know, the cost of living continues to increase. If you live longer, you're going to need more money. That's just one more reason not to make a rash decision when it comes to claiming Social Security. A related factor is your health. If you have existing health issues or potential health issues, we want to take those into account also. Retirement involves more than just your money, which is why it's essential to take a comprehensive approach to planning that brings all of these pieces together. The Retirement Shield helps address these areas and puts them together in an easy-to-understand way, so you'll know that your family is protected and safe.

Spousal Benefits

Another critical factor to consider is spousal benefits. All of the decisions about retirement are choices that married couples need to make together. This is true not only with regard to Social Security but also with pensions if you have one. When we meet with clients, we talk a lot about spousal benefits. We deal firsthand with many widows and widowers, and we are always surprised by how many people overlook this issue in their planning. The fact is that there are two people at a table planning for retirement, but most likely, there will be only one person at that table dealing with retirement.

If you do get a pension, how much will your spouse receive if you die? Will he or she receive any of it? In the case of Social Security, the surviving spouse collects the higher of the Social Security benefits, meaning that if both partners are drawing benefits and one passes away, the survivor receives the higher of the two monthly Social Security checks, not both. That means an immediate loss of income for the surviving spouse. If there is no pension, or if the spouse is not going to receive any of the pension, then it's especially important to make sure to get the most you can from the remaining Social Security benefit.

The following story illustrates the importance of making these decisions together as a couple.

Gary and Julia married when they were in their early twenties. Gary worked for the state government his whole life and retired at age 62 with a phenomenal pension. He and Julia were the same age, and they both decided to collect Social Security early at age 62 when Gary retired. Every month they had his pension check and both of their Social Security checks, which gave them plenty of money.

Unfortunately, Gary passed away at age 70, and suddenly Julia was left with a considerable drop in income. She only received half of his pension and lost her own Social Security check — remember, the surviving spouse receives only the larger of the couple's two checks — so her financial situation changed dramatically.

The irony was that Gary didn't even need to start taking his Social Security because he had a pension. By collecting Social Security early, he took a significant reduction in his benefit. After he passed away, Julia was only getting $1,000 a month instead of the $2,200 that she would have received if Gary had delayed taking his Social Security to age 70. That's a big difference, which could have been uncovered had they created a Retirement Shield for their family.

Gary passed away earlier than anybody would have imagined. But if he had delayed his Social Security until age 70, the difference in his monthly benefit would have replaced the amount of pension that Julia lost. They didn't need the money; the only reason that they opted to collect Social

Security at age 62 was that they thought they had to upon retiring. This type of misinformation is costing Americans hundreds of thousands of dollars in lost income and adds unnecessary stress in your retirement years.

Julia not only lost her husband but also suffered a tremendous financial loss. That loss could have been avoided if someone had helped them in the beginning by saying, "No, no. Don't turn on Social Security. Let it grow because you don't need that income right now. Then if you pass away, the amount of money that you would have collected at age 70 will pass to your wife, and that will bridge the income gap. That would more than replace the pension."

People so often make these decisions without realizing the implications. In this case, both longevity and spousal benefits played a considerable role. Just a little bit of simple advice would have made a big difference for Julia.

Keep Working

A third factor to consider in deciding about Social Security is whether you will continue to work. We get a lot of questions from people about the possibility of continuing to work while collecting Social Security benefits. This is partially due to people living longer and being healthier. Some people enjoy their work and want to continue working into their retirement years, either full or part time. Others find new careers or decide to start a new business post-retirement.

Those decisions have implications for your Social Security benefits, and there are some restrictions on how you can claim them. For instance, if you want to claim your benefits before full retirement age, the government places a limit on how much money you can earn in that calendar year without having your benefits affected. If you decide to claim in the year you will reach your full retirement age, you have to time it correctly because there's a limit there also. Once you reach full retirement age, there's no limit. Understanding the timing and these limits can make a significant impact on how you live in retirement.

If you do want to keep working, that's something for us to discuss. What would that look like? How much can you earn before you incur a major penalty? If you make too much money, you could be looking at a 30% to 50% penalty on your earnings that could cause a portion of your benefits to be withheld. That's why we have to get into the details of what you want in retirement so you can maximize your Social Security.

We recently talked with Corey and Wendy, who are great clients. Corey was planning to turn on his Social Security benefits six months before his full retirement age. That meant he had a limit on how much he could earn and would have potentially incurred a one-third penalty on his excess earnings, causing a reduction in his benefits, and, in his case, he didn't even need to activate the benefit. It was just a date that he and his broker had decided on.

Continuing to work may be the best option if you're healthy and you want to keep working, but you can't just take your benefit whenever you feel like it. If Corey chose to file six months prior to his full retirement age and continued to work in excess of the earnings limit, he would have incurred a one-third reduction in his benefits based on his excess income. All he had to do was wait until he reached his full retirement month, and then he would have had no earnings limit and no reduction in benefits.

Another significant factor that people often overlook in discussing Social Security is the potential tax implications on the benefits themselves.

If you make over a certain amount as a single filer or a couple filing jointly, there are tax implications that require you to pay taxes on up to 85% of your benefit amount. Again, we can't just wing it on such an important decision. We must consider multiple factors to ensure maximization of your Social Security for you and your family's plan.

This is absolutely different for everybody, and it can change rapidly and often. One common question is, "What if I start collecting Social Security at full retirement age, but then go back to work?" If that's the case for you, it may affect your monthly benefit, and it may cause some of your benefits to be subject to taxes. There are windows of opportunity where you can maximize it and fly under the radar. The reality is that it doesn't take a lot of other income to cause a portion of Social Security benefits to become taxable, but there are strategies that can help mitigate that risk if proper planning is done ahead of time. The complexity of this system and the nature of your individual situation make it essential for you to talk with someone who can help you understand the implications and create a reliable plan that works for your family.

Bruce and Paula's Horror Story

This real-life horror story about these tax implications was relayed to us by one of the couples who attended a recent Retirement Shield class.

Bruce and Paula own some rental property that is part of a little neighborhood. Just last year, the residents all voted to repave the streets, and everyone had to pay their share of the cost. Bruce and Paula needed about $15,000 *to chip in their piece. So they called their broker, and he said, "No problem. You have a CD coming due. I'll wire you the money next week." They were thrilled. But at the end of the year, they got a notice that the money they took out was IRA money, and they now owed taxes on it.*

They ended up having to pay income tax on the IRA withdrawal. Because of the additional taxable income from the IRA, they also had to pay taxes on their Social Security for the first time in their retirement. Some simple planning would have saved them from having to pay thousands of dollars in taxes. But once again, no one told them that. No one walked them through the process of deciding how best to access the money they needed. So they ended up paying taxes on their Social Security benefit when they could have just taken money out of their checking account and never missed a beat.

The result was thousands of dollars' worth of taxation just because no one looked at tax implications for the Social Security benefit. Where you pull your money from and how you pull your money makes a big difference. Bruce and Paula could have used that money, but, instead, they paid it to the government. It was a simple mistake that had more significant consequences than they ever imagined.

We've been talking about all of this in terms of couples, but planning is essential for single people as well. As a single person, you don't have anybody else to fall back on in terms of pensions or nest eggs. And in terms of tax implications, a single person has a lower earnings limit. A lot of our clients are single women, so the one thing we always do is ensure that their money is paying them back and that there's a lot of security within their plan because once you make one of these decisions, there's no going back.

Your bank or your broker may not be able to give you the correct answer. They tell you to call Social Security, where you're on hold for an hour. The people in the Social Security call center are not paid to give you an answer that considers your specific circumstances; they're paid to give you an answer, get you off the phone, and answer the next phone call. When they do give you an answer, it's generic — not custom-tailored to your unique situation. They are not financial advisors, so you can't really blame them. They're just doing their job. As Retirement Shield coaches, our job is to ask the right questions and help our clients navigate their retirement in the best way possible. That's why we build long-term relationships with our clients because we know that even seemingly small decisions can have a significant impact.

All of that means there's a lot of misinformation out there, and it's why studies show that 96% of Americans don't claim Social Security at the right time. We want you to be in the 4%. That's why we've written this book, and it's why we are happy to meet with you and discuss your unique situation. Your retirement is too important to leave it to chance.

When we work with clients through the Retirement Shield process, we always look at the full picture. It's never Social Security by itself. It's what's going on in the full retirement picture. We look at longevity, your income need, your family dynamic, and your nest egg. We look at every piece of the puzzle, and Social Security is just one of those pieces.

When we teach our Social Security classes, we go through everything discussed in this chapter, and at the end, we ask, "Okay, who realizes you can maximize this, but you can no longer wing it?" and everybody raises their hand. We hope that by reading this book, you now have this same understanding.

Social Security is one of those things that people think they understand. The reality is that most people don't realize how much they don't know. It's a complex system and is a vital part of your Retirement Shield.

Most people think Social Security is a no-brainer. But when you get down to it, and you realize how many things go into making the correct decision to maximize your benefit and avoid paying penalties on your own money — it's astounding. When you think about all the loopholes and all the caveats involved in claiming something that's yours by right, well, you know it must be tricky if 96% of Americans get it wrong. Most people have no idea how complicated it is.

When most people start thinking about collecting Social Security, they are only thinking about the next month and how much that check will be. They seldom project it out the way they should. If longevity is significant in your family — and remember, just in general, people are living longer than ever before — and you have just enough money to get by now, what's it going to be like in 10 or 15 years?

In our class, we use the example of Jean, who is considering retirement. If she opts into Social Security at age 62, she gets $1,000 a month, and she thinks that's great. She says, "If I wait until age 66, it only goes to $1,500," and most people in the class say, "Well, that's not a very big jump." But then there's always one lady who says, "Well, actually, it's a good amount of money. It's $500 a month. That's $6,000 over a year, and over 10 years, that's $60,000 in benefits. My husband and I could do a lot of traveling with $60,000." Until you make that money tangible, you don't think of it as that big a difference. And if Jean waits till age 70, instead of getting $1,000 a month, she'll get $1,800, so her benefit almost doubles in eight years.

Over a lifetime of benefits, that $600 or $900 a month is hundreds of thousands of dollars. At first glance, it may not seem like that's a big deal, but people aren't projecting or thinking about the rest of their life. They're just thinking about now. They say, "Oh, it'd be nice to have an extra $1,000 or $1,500 a month," but nobody is thinking about interest rates. Nobody's thinking about inflation. If inflation is what we believe it will be, then $1,000 today won't be $1,000 in 10 years. It's going to take $1,300 or $1,400 to make that same $1,000, and people just don't think about that. Whether it's the political climate, interest rates, or inflation, these are the things you have to think about as you consider your retirement.

If your nest egg, or the retirement income you have, is good and strong for right now, then don't turn on Social Security, because you will need that additional income over the next 10 to 15 years. That's not a guess. It's proven. Doesn't it cost you more to go to the grocery store now than it did 10 years ago?

Anyone who is contemplating retirement can remember what prices were like when they first started working. Remember when you could get a gallon of gas for 25 cents?

Inflation will affect your retirement income. When and how you begin taking your Social Security benefit will play a significant role in your standard of living, your level of stress, and your overall satisfaction in your retirement years. Make the right decision and talk with someone who can help you create your Retirement Shield so your family will be protected for life.

A goal without a plan is just a wish.

~ Antoine de Saint-Exupéry

Chapter 4

Income Shield

Throughout your working life, you take home a regular paycheck. It may be every week, every two weeks, or once a month, but you know that during those 30 or 40 years while you're working, you have a consistent, predictable amount of income. These are what we call the accumulation years, the part of your financial life when, ideally, you are building up resources for the day when you are no longer working.

Then that long-awaited day arrives. You retire, and all of a sudden, that regular paycheck stops, which can be a pretty scary prospect. Some people even keep working because they are fearful of retirement.

After all, your regular monthly expenses don't stop, so you still need an income. How are you going to replace that steady paycheck to maintain your standard of living? You are moving into the next stage of your financial life, going from the accumulation years into the distribution years.

Once you stop working, you're not going to have an additional accumulation of cash, and you're not going to be contributing to your retirement accounts any longer. When you retire, you usually stop saving because you don't have the income to do that anymore.

This is a huge change in your life. And yet, this is the part most Americans don't think about or plan for. Statistics tell us that 95% of Americans — whether they're already retired or are going to retire in the next six to 10 years — don't have a plan to provide themselves with income in their retirement. They have no written income plan or distribution plan.

You have worked hard for 30 or 40 years. How do you take what you have acquired during those years and guarantee yourself security in your retirement?

If you take nothing else from this book, remember this: YOU NEED A PLAN.

The Three-Legged Race

For many years, most people tended to work for the same company for most, if not all, of their working life. We all know of people who worked 20, 30, or 40 years or more for the same organization. They were likely to retire with a gold watch and a pension. That pension was a key component of the traditional model of retirement. It was reminiscent of a three-legged race that many of us played in grade school. Others have referred to these three components as the three-legged stool of retirement.

The three legs of the stool were 1) your pension, 2) your Social Security, and 3) your savings or nest egg as it's often called. But retirement has changed from our parents' and grandparents' days. That three-legged stool has all but disappeared.

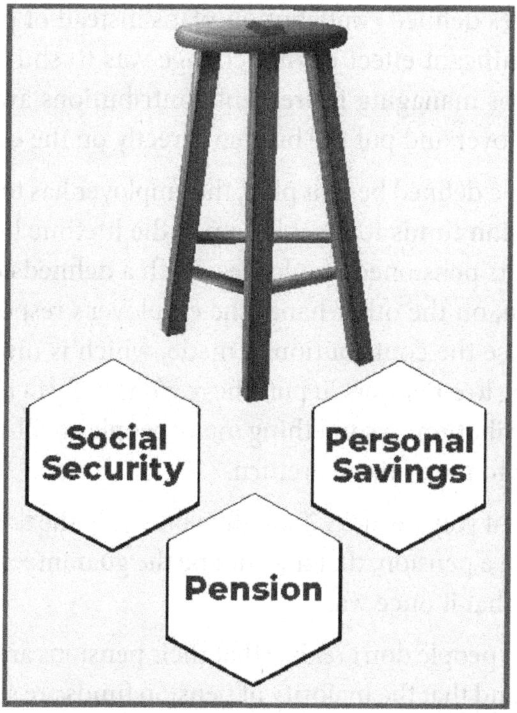

A Different Model

Today, few Americans stay with the same company for their entire career. According to a 2019 study by the Bureau of Labor Statistics, Baby Boomers in America hold an average of 12 jobs throughout their lifetime. So few Americans stay with a single company long enough to earn a pension, even if the company offers one, which fewer and fewer companies do.

Over the past several decades, thanks to legislative changes and other factors, companies have mostly shifted from offering defined benefit plans (also known as pensions) to offering defined contribution plans (typically a 401(k) or 403(b) account). The 401(k) goes back to the early '80s during the Reagan administration, when changes in the law made it more attractive and economical for employers to offer their employees defined contribution plans instead of pensions. One significant effect of that change was to shift responsibility for managing retirement contributions away from the employer and put the burden directly on the employee.

With a defined benefit plan, the employer has to manage the pension funds to be able to pay the lifetime benefits it owes to its pensioned employees. With a defined contribution plan, on the other hand, the employer's responsibility stops once the contribution is made, which is much more appealing to employers. It puts the responsibility of managing the contribution — something many people are ill-prepared to do — to maximize its return.

Even if you are lucky enough to be one of the few Americans with a pension, that may not be the guaranteed lifetime income that it once was.

Most people don't realize that their pensions aren't guaranteed, and that the majority of pension funds are struggling because of low interest rates. That's another reason a lot of companies have frozen or done away with their pension plans altogether. They are no longer able to accumulate enough money within the plans to stay 100% solvent. Many people believe that employer pension programs will be insolvent within a few years. In other words, just because you have a pension now doesn't mean you always will.

It's also important to understand that if you do have a pension, it doesn't just kick in automatically upon your retirement. You need to make decisions about when and how to take your pension — just as you do about when and how you take your Social Security.

For example, one of the biggest mistakes we see when someone is claiming a pension is deciding how to take a spousal benefit. The purpose of the spousal benefit is to protect your spouse in the event of your death. When you take a spousal benefit, you take a lower monthly payment so that your spouse will continue to receive your pension if you pass away first. If you claim a traditional spousal benefit, it can be the most expensive benefit that you'll ever pay for, and you may or may not use it. If you claim the spousal benefit and your spouse passes away before you do, you took a reduction in benefits for no reason. If you both live a very long time, you also accepted a benefit reduction for no reason.

There's an art (and some math) involved in selecting the right survivor benefit to ensure that you're getting the best of both worlds. The point of the spousal benefit is not only to protect your spouse but also to protect the household from losing income. Part of the Retirement Shield process is walking through pension decisions with our clients and making sure they are adequately protected and their household does not lose income.

Planning Your Retirement Income

Retirement today is not what it was decades ago. What that means is that if you are like most Americans, you are in charge of your retirement.

The demise of the traditional three-legged stool means that today, most Americans have only a two-legged stool: Social Security — which is why it's so important to maximize that benefit — and your retirement nest egg, consisting of your IRA, 401(k), 403(b) and whatever savings you may have.

The advantage of the three-legged stool was diversification. With only two legs of the stool remaining, it's even more critical to make the most of those assets through both growth and protection. By the time you reach the typical retirement age of 65 or 66 years old, you don't have time on your side to weather any financial storms and rebuild your assets, and it becomes critically important to protect and preserve what you have. Again, you need a plan.

When you retire, you want to know that on the 15th of every month, there's money going into your account, just as it was when you were working. That's why we sit down and customize your retirement income plan as a true distribution plan. We talk about what you want your retirement years to look like, and we determine how best to meet your financial needs and wants. We ask questions, such as:

- Will you need a newer car in the next 10 to 15 years?
- Have you always wanted to spend your retirement years traveling? Maybe you've always wanted to see foreign lands, or perhaps you have loved ones in other states that you hope to visit.
- Will you be traveling across the country to spend time with kids and grandkids?

All of the above are wonderful ideas and goals, but how are you going to pay for them? Where's that money coming from? Your plan will answer those questions.

Other Considerations

And there are other considerations. Life doesn't always follow the plan, so it's crucial to prepare for the unexpected as much as possible. We discuss the difficult questions that need to be addressed and answered in a true distribution plan, such as:

- What if the markets go down 30%?
- Can you live on 30% less each month?

- What if inflation goes up 4% or 5%?
- Will you just start taking out more money?

Planning Pays Off

We met Donna and Sam shortly after they married, a second marriage for both of them. Though marriage can be challenging at times, the more significant hurdle for them was the mounting medical bills they were facing due to complications from Sam's surgery. They were unsure when he would fully recover or if he would need long-term care assistance. Since financial planning was not their strong suit, they reached out to us to see how to protect the money they had saved for retirement from being spent on medical bills or lost in a market correction. To say they were a bit stressed is an understatement.

Once we heard their story and clearly understood their unique situation, we were able to put their hearts at ease. Together, we created a Retirement Shield that gave them the protection they desired. The first step was to protect the money they had saved. We were able to do this so they would avoid any loss when the market corrected (which it did just a few weeks after we met). You've never seen a bigger smile than when Donna realized she had not lost a penny while those around her were losing thousands. She was very relieved and felt fabulous.

Next, we turned our attention to the income side of their plan. Donna and Sam wanted to make certain they would have money to live on for the rest of their lives, regardless of the mounting medical bills that were coming their way. Using a Retirement Shield strategy, we put in place an income plan that provides them with what they need to live on for the rest of their lives. Never again will they need to concern themselves with where the money is going to come from or if it will be there. They go to sleep every night knowing they can live out the rest of their years as they've always dreamed they would.

Finally, we made sure they had proper long-term care protection in case either of them needed to move in this direction. Unlike many policies of this type, which are extremely expensive, we integrated this coverage into their Retirement Shield plan so that it's available should they need it yet doesn't deplete their retirement savings or income. The peace of mind this part of their plan gives them is priceless.

Kris M. Retirement Shield coach in California

Life can throw us curve balls. Whether that comes in the form of a market correction, an unforeseen medical situation, or the reality of needing long-term care assistance, we need to prepare for these possibilities sooner rather than later. Donna and Sam are in a happy place now because they didn't wait until it was too late. They realized what could happen and took action to protect themselves.

It's never too late to start. At the same time, there's no reason to delay. Have a conversation with your Retirement Shield coach and create a plan to protect your future regardless of what life throws your way.

Establishing a Distribution Plan

Your distribution plan clearly outlines where all of your money is coming from throughout your retirement years. Once that plan is established, you'll know where the money for your travel is coming from. You'll be confident that if and when the market corrects, things will be okay because you have planned for everything that could or will happen. The one thing we know for sure is that life's going to happen.

The market usually corrects every three to four years, so we have to plan for these things. What happens if inflation goes up? What happens if interest rates go up? What happens if there's a terrorist attack? The markets usually don't like those things. How is that going to affect your family? How is that going to affect your monthly income?

By having a true distribution plan in place, you will be able to eliminate the worry and fear that can eat away at your peace of mind. You will be able to approach your retirement with confidence because you have a comprehensive plan that has been stress tested. You will know what to expect if the markets correct or even if there is a major terrorist attack. Instead of losing 30%–50% in a market downturn, you will be able to preserve your money and rely on the plan you have in place.

Your plan should project into the future and anticipate an increase in inflation as well as address any medical issues that might arise. If you need a newer car, that's in the plan. If you want to travel once a year for $5,000, $6,000, or $8,000, that's in the plan. We can tweak your plan and get it to work within the parameters of the money you have.

Some people might say, "Hey, you know what? We really want $6,500 a month." Well, we'll put that in the plan, look at the numbers, and we might say, "$6,500 is stretching it.

$6,200 is a lot more reasonable." Other people say, "We really want $5,000 or $7,000 a month." Our response may be, "That's probably not attainable if we go through a major correction. You have enough money now to do the things you want to do, but you cannot afford a major correction in the market. We need to take steps to make sure you don't lose 30% or 40%."

These days, there are many questions about America and its financial future. That's why it's more important than ever not to wing it with your retirement plan. Your retirement plan can be affected by factors you might not even see coming, maybe even things that America has never dealt with before.

Take Social Security, for example. As we said in the last chapter, Social Security is probably the closest thing to a guaranteed pension-like payment that most people will ever have for their own lifetime and that of their spouse.

When Social Security began, and retirement planning started, there were five workers for every person receiving a benefit. But the number of workers per retiree has dropped significantly. We're down to two workers for every one person who receives a benefit.

Today, there are three to four times more people claiming Social Security benefits than we have in the workforce. That's never happened before. It's almost turned upside down. We used to have more contributions going in than we had people taking money out. But now we have more people taking withdrawals as the Baby Boomers retire than we have people in the workforce. That's a little scary, and it's why most people believe by 2030 or so, there will be a reduction in benefits because the current model cannot sustain itself.

Pensions are also facing challenges from low interest rates. Pension fund managers can't leave their money in the bank and expect to make 6%, 7% or 8% interest so they can pay out their pension obligations. Pension funds only make 1%–2% today, which means making their payments is starting to burn through their surplus. It's eating into their capital, and that's also pretty scary.

Any or all of these factors can affect your personal retirement, which is why — say it with me now! — YOU NEED A PLAN.

Along with these outside factors, we help our clients look at longevity, survivor benefits, and taxation. We teach our clients to consider the legacy they want to pass on to future generations. All of these things play a role in a Retirement Shield plan. We create a plan that addresses similar situations but maximizes the money, whether it's Social Security, pension, or income planning. Each one of these elements needs to be looked at individually, but they all play off of each other as well. Not having a plan could set you up for failure. You've probably heard the saying, "No one plans to fail, but people fail to plan." That's the difference.

Too often, couples don't discuss these things. We have often sat down with a widow who expects to receive all or a good portion of their spouse's pension. Our hearts sink when we see how they didn't plan well, and that expectation gets demolished. What they discover is that instead of the $1,500 or $1,800 a month they were anticipating, the pension drops to zero. Or instead of receiving $3,000 a month, they're only going to get $1,500. That's a real jolt for anyone, but especially for someone who has just suffered the loss of a spouse. This is the problem with not having a plan.

Some of the old-timers made their pension decisions without their wives, sometimes not making any provisions for their wives. These days, a spouse has to sign off on the pension distribution plan, which is good, but it doesn't always happen. A lot of people don't even understand what they're signing or know how to make the best decision.

Another critical piece of your retirement plan is your legacy. People often tell me, "Hey, we want to leave money to our kids and our grandkids." Well, how do you do that without a plan?

Taxation comes into play as well. Where your retirement money comes from affects how much you pay in taxes today and how much you'll pay in taxes down the road. A healthy distribution plan digs into all the pieces of the puzzle to make sure you can leave as much money behind as you want. Legacy planning is incredibly important, but you can't do it without a distribution plan — because without a plan, you're just going to burn through money, and you won't have any money left.

The Retirement Shield is a process that helps address each of these areas. Going through the process, you could have the peace of mind knowing that you have a blueprint of your future that protects those you love and provides for the life you most want to live. You've worked hard to build up your nest egg, now is the time to protect it by going through the Retirement Shield process.

Margaret's Rash Decision

We are passionate about helping people create their retirement plan because we've heard too many heartbreaking stories. Margaret became a widow when her husband James *died prematurely from cancer. James had a pension, but Margaret's options for receiving his pension were limited. She could only choose from among a set number of payouts instead of a lifetime benefit. She was led to believe that her only real option was a 10-year payout. Margaret took the 10-year payout, and that ran out a couple of years ago. The truth was that she did have other options, but she hadn't explored them. It's a common story: a widow making an income decision for a 10-year period of time that will affect her life forever. This decision has created about a $15,000 to $18,000 shortage of income in her retirement, and it didn't have to be that way.*

Margaret made a rash decision in talking to her husband's union. They encouraged her to choose the option she did, but she had other options that would have provided for her better. Instead of running out of money, she could have had plenty of money for the rest of her life.

Margaret's story clearly shows why you don't want to make rash decisions. You want to talk with a professional. You want to have a plan for how your money is going to work and last. The goal of having a plan is so that your money can pay you back. You worked hard to accumulate it. Now it's time for you to stop working and let the money to pay you back.

How do you get there? How do you make that happen? You do that through a distribution plan. You do it through thinking about what may happen and planning for it. You do it through walking through any kind of market scenario or political atmosphere to make sure that you can weather those storms.

We have heard way too many widow stories that start with, "I thought I was going to get his $1,800-a-month pension. I lost my $900 Social Security check. I get his $1,500

Social Security check, but I lost the pension and my Social Security check. So I'm short about $2,400 a month. What do I do?" That often means selling the house or burning through other assets, but if there had just simply been a plan in place, we wouldn't be burning through assets. We wouldn't be in a position where we have to make drastic changes.

We know certain things are going to happen over the next 15 or 20 years. There will be different presidents, shifting political climates, changes in the tax structure, and multiple market corrections. But having a plan in place ensures that when those things happen, we're good. Everything we do in life has a plan, but for some reason, retirement doesn't. That's hard to understand but simple to change.

Always plan ahead. It wasn't raining when Noah built the ark.

~ Richard Cushing

Chapter 5

Tax Shield

There's an old saying, often attributed to Benjamin Franklin, that goes like this: "In this world, nothing can be said to be certain except death and taxes."

It's still true. Taxes are one of those inevitabilities of life. No one wants to talk about them, but we all know that they're going to happen. So what do we do about that? By now, you won't be surprised to hear that what we need is a plan.

What we need to do is be proactive. Sitting back and being reactive won't solve the issue.

While taxes are inevitable, they don't stay constant. There have been significant changes in taxation in recent years, and there are certainly more changes to come. How do we know that? Look at where our tax dollars go.

Over the last couple of years, studies have shown that 66 cents of every dollar we give the government has gone to fund four major items: Social Security, Medicare, Medicaid, and the national debt. That leaves only 34 cents of every dollar to fund over $200 trillion in unfunded liabilities. Obviously, that's not enough money, but here's what's interesting. Over the next couple of years, those four items will consume up to 92 cents of every tax dollar. That leaves the government only

8 cents on the dollar to fund over 200 trillion in unfunded liabilities, not to mention the shortfall of Social Security.

This issue is incredibly important. Taxes are the most significant time bomb of retirement, and no one's discussing them.

At some point, something has to change, and here's what we know: People aren't going to run for office on a promise to cut your benefits. No candidate is going to say, "Vote for me. I'm going to lower your Social Security." That's not how it works.

This projected shortfall of money means that taxes are going to increase down the road. It's not a matter of if but a matter of when. That's why we need to be talking about this and planning for it.

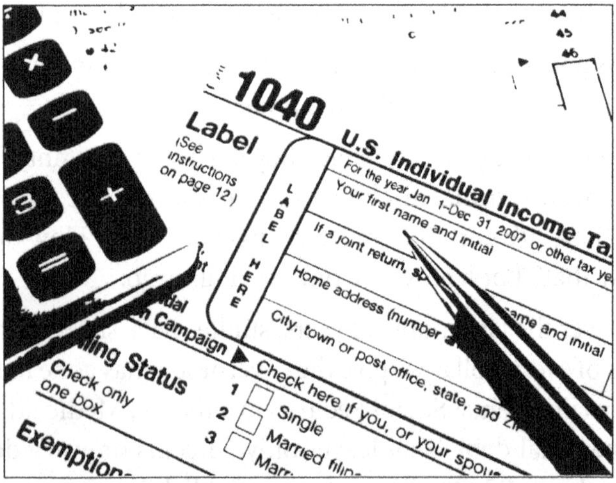

The Tax Time Bomb

You've been led to assume that when you retire, your taxes will be lower because your income will be lower. That seems reasonable, doesn't it? The trouble is that it's not that simple. Reality can turn that assumption upside down.

In the last chapter, we talked about the fact that traditional pensions have largely been replaced by 401(k) or 403(b) accounts. Today, most Americans have a good portion of their retirement assets in IRAs, 401(k)s, or 403(b)s. In fact, we could call the Baby Boomer generation the 401(k) generation.

What do all these accounts have in common? They are tax-deferred accounts. During your working years, you put pre-tax dollars straight from your paycheck into these accounts, with the idea that by the time you have retired and start withdrawing that money, you will be in a lower tax bracket. You still owe taxes on that money; you have only deferred — in essence, postponed — paying those taxes until you retire.

Here's the catch. You don't just owe taxes on the money you have contributed to your tax-deferred account. You owe taxes on all of it — every penny you've put in, every penny that was employer-matched, and every penny of growth. It's all taxable.

What does that mean in terms of real numbers? Let's look at an example. Suppose you have worked 30 years and have put $75,000 into your 401(k). That's what the government has allowed you to do by putting in a certain amount each year. Over the years, you have deferred paying taxes on $75,000 of your salary by contributing $100 or $200 out of each paycheck to your 401(k). And your employer has a match program, putting in a dollar for each one you contribute. That makes $150,000 in total contributions to that 401(k). Now, let's suppose the account has done very well in terms of growth, so by the time you are ready to retire, the account is worth $300,000. That's a nice nest egg, right?

Chances are no one bothered to mention to you that this nest egg could be a tax liability down the road.

Here you are, facing retirement. You've stashed all this money away. You're part of what we call the 401(k) generation. As we explained, pensions started going away in the '80s when corporate America realized they could save money by opting to offer defined contribution plans such as 401(k)s. These tax-deferred options might have seemed like a huge benefit for employees. Still, the government knew all along that, eventually, they would be taxing a more considerable amount at what would most likely be a higher tax margin.

When we look at the government and tax policy today, we expect taxes to go up. Anticipating that taxes could go up as much as 15% to 20% over the next few years, retirement prospects change drastically. As with everything we've discussed so far, all the pieces of the puzzle have to fit together to create your Retirement Shield. So what happens if we now have to take an extra 15% to 20% off the top of your nest egg?

The average American family would lose $800 to $1,000 a month in buying power, and most are on a restricted income. They're retired and on a fixed income. Remember, retirement is about distribution, not accumulation. That retirement income is not going to go up all of a sudden to pay for higher taxes, which is why it's so important to be proactive in identifying things that can hurt your retirement before they happen. Part of that is planning for tax changes.

You can either plan proactively, lower that tax burden, and protect your hard-earned money, or wait for that tax bomb to explode, and pay away most of your money into taxes that you could have prevented.

No one likes to talk about this because the right planning takes time and effort. The big bank has no interest in doing that; they're interested in babysitting your money. If you ask your advisor or the big bank a tax question, they're going to tell you that they're not a CPA. Then when you go to your CPA and ask them your tax questions, they will most likely say, "Well, I'm not a financial advisor." If any of these people do give you tax advice, chances are it will be conflicting advice, and, usually, one or two of them are incorrect about what you can and should do. This illustrates yet another reason that you need a financial professional who can help you develop a comprehensive retirement plan that includes tax planning. It's also one of the primary reasons we created the Retirement Shield process — so you can get help putting together your own comprehensive retirement plan.

Tax Reduction Opportunities

Here's the good news. What most people don't realize is that they have time on their side to reduce their tax burden in retirement. And some recent changes in the law have made that easier.

Congress passed the Setting Every Community Up for Retirement Enhancement (SECURE) Act and signed it into law in December 2019. The law took effect at the beginning of 2020, offering some important advantages for retirement planning. One of the most significant changes is the increase in the age for the required minimum distribution (RMD) from tax-deferred accounts. Until now, the law required you to begin taking your RMD at age 70 1/2. The SECURE Act raises the RMD age to 72, giving you a year and a half longer to take action to reduce your tax liability before you have to start drawing funds from your IRA or 401(k).

That's a real benefit, and you want to take advantage of it as soon as possible. We've already noted that taxes are likely to increase. Eventually, the government will probably also increase the amount of the RMD that you have to pull out of the IRA.

We can anticipate that and do something about it. One way to do that is by converting funds to a Roth account, which is a tax-free account. Your typical advisor, however, doesn't make money moving your money from portfolio A to portfolio B. They only make money on new money. That means they're constantly trying to get people to contribute to their Roth account, not convert existing funds to the Roth. But by doing Roth conversions, getting proactive, and having a tax plan in place, the average American family can lower taxation by $60,000 to $100,000 in retirement. That means more money to take care of yourself and your family, more money to deal with inflation, more money to pass on for legacy, and more money to provide for assisted living or long-term health care.

The whole point of the Retirement Shield is to have a process in place to protect our clients' retirements and their nest eggs from the things that could potentially hurt it or harm it. That's why we take taxes so seriously.

Terry and Joe's Explosion

Terry and Joe have been retired for several years. They own some rental property, and a couple of years ago, they needed to make some major repairs on one of their rentals. They called their financial advisor, who said, "No problem. You have an investment coming due in the next few weeks, and it should cover the repair bill."

Terry and Joe said, "Great. Just transfer the money to our bank account." The advisor transferred the money, Terry and Joe made the repairs, and everything seemed fine. Then, at the end of the year, they got a notification that the money had come out of a qualified (tax-deferred) plan. So they had to pay taxes on that money that was taxed as ordinary income. To make matters much worse, the money they had withdrawn put them into a higher tax bracket, so they also had to pay taxes on their Social Security for the first time since they retired. This tax bomb surprised them, and the aftereffects took a toll on their savings.

The tax liability was the result of taking the money from the wrong account. If the financial advisor had pulled the funds from their nonqualified account, no taxes would have been due, and there wouldn't have been a trickle-down effect on their Social Security. Terry and Joe's story shows how important it is to understand where your money is coming from. The type of account the money comes from will affect how and when that money is taxed.

In looking at your distribution plan, you must consider all the different things that you're going to need and want to do with your money. But, remember, if you don't pull money out of the right bucket, you may unknowingly increase your taxes for no reason. And no one wants to pay more in unnecessary taxes. But that's what happens when you don't have a plan.

Let's look at Mark and Peggy's situation. Mark is almost 66 years old and has been contributing to his IRA plan for over 45 years. Over the last 10 years or so, his advisor never suggested that Mark should start preparing for retirement by initiating a Roth IRA and reducing his contributions to his taxable account. When Mark retires, all of the money in his IRA will be taxable. He'll lose a lot of money to taxes — money that he and Peggy could have used and enjoyed if they had a plan and an advisor who understood all of these issues. There's no reason to put all of your money into a tax-deferred account. The benefit of a Roth IRA is that every penny you put in and every penny of growth is eventually nontaxable. If you've been building a nest egg of taxable money, wouldn't it be nice to have a pile of money that's not taxable?

Suppose you and your spouse want to take a trip. Wouldn't it be great to be able to take that money out of an account that's not taxable? Suppose you need a new roof, or you have a family emergency. Wouldn't you prefer to be able to pull money that's not taxable? This is why a tax plan is so important. Most of the time, there's a 15% to 20% reduction in taxation over your retirement simply by getting the plan in place and doing the work. It's your money, and you need a plan to protect it. The Retirement Shield could be a part of helping you put together that plan.

Practical Strategies

People say they want to reduce their taxes, but they often don't understand the steps they can take to lower them in retirement.

One of the best strategies to lower taxation is to convert your IRA money into a Roth IRA, which is never taxable, provided certain conditions are met. You generally shouldn't convert all at once because you would trigger a tax tsunami, but with careful planning, you can make your money nontaxable.

There's a limit to how much you can contribute to a Roth each year, but there is no limit to how much money you can convert because you pay tax on that money at the time of conversion. If you convert prior to age 59 1/2, you won't pay a penalty on the converted amount as long as you wait at least five years before withdrawing it. With that in mind, you can carefully plan your conversions many years before your anticipated need for the money.

When you start converting funds to a Roth, you need to have a strategy in place to do it over time. You don't want to start jumping tax brackets and paying more taxes than necessary. For instance, let's say that you're single filer and that you claim $25,000 a year. Assuming your next tax bracket is $50,000, each year, you could convert $25,000 of IRA money, paying your 12 percent tax. Putting that $25,000 into a Roth allows it to grow tax-free, as long as you wait at least five years before withdrawing that growth. We know that taxes are going to increase eventually, so why not convert your money now instead of later? At some point, you'll be forced to pull money out of the tax-deferred account, and taxes will be higher, so you'll be paying more taxes than necessary. Even if you converted only $10,000 each year, you'd still be ahead because you'd be paying 12% on $10,000 instead of paying 15% to 20% or more down the road.

The Widow Tax

Another critical factor that married couples don't typically discuss is the widow tax. The best way to illustrate this is to talk about Greg and Ellen. They both retired a few years ago and have both been drawing money from their IRAs. Not long ago, Greg passed away. Now Ellen has double the amount of income, but her tax filing status changes to single the year after Greg's death. So she's getting relatively the same amount of income and no longer reaps the benefit of the married filing jointly status. That means her tax thresholds reduce to a single status, and her taxes go up. Ellen didn't do anything wrong. Her taxes are going up 15% to 20% simply because she can no longer file married filing jointly.

We call this the widow tax. It's another of those things that people don't talk about, but we do. We know that, on average, men die sooner than women, and the widow will be left with less money but not so little that the widow tax will go away. Without proper planning for the widow tax, an unexpected tax result could further reduce the remaining income to the survivor spouse. Unfortunately, it's only a matter of time for most people unless they've done careful planning to avoid that situation.

Legacy Planning and Taxes

Many of the people we meet with are concerned about leaving money to their kids or, especially, their grandkids.

The quickest and best way to do that is to alleviate any tax burden in retirement. Wouldn't it be great to pass on money to the kids that's <u>never</u> taxable? With the compounding effect of growing the money and then it not being taxable, you can sometimes create three to four times more in legacy money because you're alleviating 20% to 30% in taxation. For example, on $1 million of taxable money, you're only going to pass on $600,000 or $700,000. But if it's all tax-free money, you're passing the whole $1 million on to the kids or the grandkids. Which of these scenarios sounds best? It's possible when you have the right plan.

What we usually see in a 20- to 30-year retirement plan is that you can multiply the amount of money passed on in legacy by three to four times.

Take Doug and Alice, for example. If we look at their current plan, we can see that they will pass on maybe $300,000 or $400,000 to the kids and grandkids if everything goes well and according to plan. By getting into tax planning, even considering market corrections, market volatility, and anything else that comes along, Doug and Alice could potentially instead pass along over $1 million in tax-free legacy money.

Often, people don't realize that most retirement plans that aren't designed correctly — which means including a robust tax planning component — will result in people running out of money. Tax planning shores up retirement plans to prevent shortages of funds. You can have the savviest investment professional who makes you 15% or 20% returns, but it's worthless if there's no tax plan behind it because you're going to give most of your money back to the government in taxes or lose it through market volatility if you don't have a protection plan in place.

Since the Great Depression, the market had been returning just better than 8%, until the year 2000 when it has been returning only slightly better than 5%. So why do financial advisors and banks build retirement plans around 7%, 8% or 9% rates of return? Where's that coming from, and why isn't it taking into account the next major correction?

What happens when the market goes backward 30% or 40%? What if we have a decline of 5% to 7% for a couple of years? History tells us the market goes up and down every three to four years, and history repeats itself, which is why we need to learn from it. The fact that we have been on this fantastic run for more than 12 years doesn't mean it's going to last forever.

Most of you reading this book will either retire within the next three to five years or have just retired within the last three to five years. Well, who wants to be forced to go back to work? The same people who want to pay more in taxes — no one!

That's why a proactive relationship with your money is the only relationship that makes any sense and is what differentiates Retirement Shield advisors from other advisors. We take a proactive approach to retirement planning and talk about the topics others don't. Why? Because we know they are going to affect you, and we want you to have a reliable plan in place before bad things happen. Through the Retirement Shield planning process, we'll discuss with you all of these areas and create a customized plan for your unique situation. It's not as complicated as it sounds when you have a reliable guide.

Maybe legacy isn't your concern. Maybe you say, "Okay, I'm not really worried about leaving a bunch of money to the kids. I'm worried about taking care of myself and my wife. We're 70 years old, and we don't have any long-term health care. We might need that money down the road."

Depending on your circumstances, you may want or need more tax diversification by holding some after-tax funds as well as tax free and tax postponed accounts. Tax diversification is more important than ever. Are you even aware that under the current tax code, you can spend your IRA dollars tax free if you use the money for health care? So many people are missing this tax deduction and paying unnecessary taxes.

Here's an example of what I mean: Many people who may need $8,000 a month to pay for nursing home expenses are told by their advisors to take out $11,000 in order to cover the taxes! That's because most advisors don't understand the tax code. Most advisors are really investment advisors, not financial planners. Too many people have over paid taxes and ran out of money long before they needed to.

That's why you need a plan.

It's time for your money to be working for you, not against you. Money is a tool. The more you have of it, the more you can bless and take care of others, including yourself. We've helped clients get their money doing what it needs to do, the way it needs to be doing it. Sitting down with a Retirement Shield coach could help spark the first steps to doing that for your retirement. Let's sit down and begin creating your Retirement Shield plan.

Someone's sitting in the shade today because someone planted a tree a long time ago.

~ *Warren Buffett*

Chapter 6

Long-Term Care Shield

Long-term care is the elephant in the room of retirement planning. No one wants to talk about it, but it's a fact of life, and no comprehensive plan can ignore it.

According to the U.S. Department of Health and Human Services, the odds of someone 65 or older requiring long-term care are about 70%. That means long-term care is going to become an issue for most everyone in some way — either for yourself or your spouse. And many of us are part of the sandwich generation, caring not only for kids and grandkids but also for parents. What happens if an elderly parent needs long-term care?

The cost of long-term care is astronomical (thousands of dollars a month), and it's not going down any time soon. Health insurance doesn't cover it. Medicare doesn't cover it. You could very well have to pay out of pocket for long-term care, and that can destroy your retirement nest egg very quickly illustrated in the following real-life example.

An Unfortunate Situation

George and Helen became clients some years ago. They were in good shape financially, with all the pieces in place, including long-term care insurance. Unfortunately, about *six months after they became clients, Helen had to go into a memory care facility. This situation is not unusual today since people are living longer than ever, and this includes people living with memory issues, dementia, or Alzheimer's. Helen has been in that facility for five years now, and their long-term care policy ran out a year ago. So every month, George writes a check for $8,000 to cover the costs for her care, and it's depleting his retirement account at a rapid pace.*

Helen could potentially live another 10 years. She has no heart issues or blood pressure issues. But the person that she was is gone and has been gone for years. Yet George is committed to caring for her, even if that costs him his last penny. It's a tragic situation for both of them.

When George and Helen first came to us, they believed that they would be fine because they had long-term care coverage. Unfortunately, most people don't understand how their long-term care works or the limits to it.

George and Helen thought they had all their bases covered, and they did, but the bases were only covered for three years. It's a sad example of what can happen when you think you have a plan in place but never really get a second opinion. These are the types of things that we review with clients to make sure they're going to be able to play the retirement game without and unexpected surprise upending their plans.

Suppose you end up living in a memory care facility; your heart and body are healthy, but your mind is gone. That kind of care can cost $7,000, $8,000, or as much as $10,000 a month. How will your family deal with that?

Are you planning for that possibility? And the bigger

question is, how are you going to pay for it? We know this is a reality of life, so what we have done is help our clients through the Retirement Shield process to include programs that include some protection against a long-term care event. Our goal is to make sure our clients don't go broke in retirement.

A Better Path Forward

Long-term care insurance isn't always the answer. With traditional long-term care policies, if you don't use the benefits, you could lose out on the premiums that you paid. We believe there's a better way to protect your family.

The cost of this insurance has gone through the roof because people are living longer than ever before. Fewer and fewer companies offer long-term care insurance. Among those that still do, premiums have been increasing dramatically over the past few years, with rates sometimes doubling in a very short time.

Fortunately, we've helped our clients choose programs that provide long-term care protection without increased rates while providing access to care if they need it. We have helped our clients gain access to insurance-related programs that provide benefits to help pay for a potential long-term care event while the cash value earns interest at a competitive rate, sometimes better than what the bank offers. One of the unique features of the program that our clients find helpful is the ability to get the original deposit made to open up a policy refunded at certain times. Ask a Retirement Shield coach for details.

There are two reasons most people don't invest in long-term care insurance:

- The high cost of the monthly premiums

- The fact that they don't want to lose all that money.

If you spend $500 a month on premiums for 10 years, that's $60,000 out of your retirement account that you're not getting back. And most people spend that money for 15 or 20 years.

Peace of Mind

Bob and Susan were in their early 60s and preparing themselves for retirement. They had scrimped and saved throughout life with the hope that they could enjoy their golden years without worrying about money. Recently, they realized that their retirement money — which was in stocks and mutual funds — was at risk and could be lost if the market had another major correction. That's when they decided to talk with us.

When we first met, they shared two of their greatest concerns: how to protect their money from loss and how to provide long-term care coverage for themselves. They had considered purchasing a long-term care policy, but the cost was too high for them. However, Bob and Susan knew that it was prudent to have this type of coverage in case one of them needed to move into an assisted living or nursing home facility. They felt stuck and didn't know what they would do until we talked.

After discussing their retirement desires and looking over their current situation, together, we created a Retirement Shield plan to meet their needs. We addressed every aspect of their retirement and focused specifically on safeguarding their money and providing proper long-term care coverage should they need it. Now their money is fully protected from any market risk, will grow as the market grows, and guarantees them a reliable income for the rest of their life.

Today, they have peace of mind knowing that should they need additional care, they have long-term care protection to rely upon. We structured their Retirement Shield in such a way that their retirement income will actually increase when they need this protection. Bob and Susan are relieved that they can pay for this care without being a burden to their family or draining their retirement savings.

Sal M.

Retirement Shield Coach in New Jersey

Bob and Susan are thrilled now that they have the protection of a Retirement Shield. They are walking into the future with full confidence that their retirement will be everything they want it to be.

That's one of the reasons we created the Retirement Shield process — so you can get the program that's going to be the best for you. Think about this: You insure everything you currently have (your house, your car, your life), except for this one piece of the puzzle. Doesn't it make sense to insure for this most probable event, especially if you can retain all of your investment if you never use it?

Using life insurance products instead of traditional long-term care insurance, we have helped our clients put a program in place that's not only affordable but offers long-term care benefits. And if some reason our clients don't use the benefit for long-term care, it could be potentially passed on to a beneficiaries.

Many traditional banks, institutions, or agents may not think to suggest these options to you. But remember, we are looking at your overall retirement plan, not just one aspect of it. As Retirement Shield coaches, we have helped our clients create a strategy that addresses long-term care events.

When we sit down and teach this type of protection plan to a client, we ensure all of the value is going to the client. The goal for the Retirement Shield is to provide our clients freedom within their retirement. This has allowed our clients use their money when they need it most.

That's why it's so important to work with a professional who specializes in the topics we have covered so far. For example, many people we've talked with continue their employer health coverage after retirement. They think that long-term care is covered. But people don't always understand their coverage, and then life happens. If you have existing coverage, it's essential to look at the limits of that coverage. Remember that Medicare does not cover long-term care — and neither does your health insurance. It's critical to make long-term care part of your overall plan.

Having proper long-term care coverage is critical not only for you but also for your children. Many times they are burdened with making these decisions with you or for you. They love you, and they will take on the role when they must, but wouldn't it be better for them and easier on them if you had a plan in place? The relief it offers to you and your family is priceless. Be sure to make long-term care part of your Retirement Shield plan.

The time to repair the roof is when the sun is shining.

~ John F. Kennedy

Chapter 7

What-If Shield

In the past several chapters, we have looked at some of the things that can threaten your retirement security. Now we get to the big question: What if? What are you going to do if the worst happens?

But first, let's look at something else that helps illustrate our point. Let me ask you another question: What do you know about that famous ship, the Titanic? I'll bet it's more than you learned by watching the movie.

Her Maiden Voyage

More than a century has passed since the RMS Titanic sank off the coast of Newfoundland in the wee hours of the morning on April 15, 1912. The ship struck an iceberg in the North Atlantic and went down, taking the lives of 1,500 people.

Other ships had sunk before it, and many others have sunk since that day, with thousands of people perishing. But why do we remember the Titanic? The ship was brand new and making its maiden voyage. At the time, it was the largest and most luxurious ship afloat. Its state-of-the-art design was described by Shipbuilder magazine as "practically unsinkable."

If this was true, then what caused it to sink? It wasn't

Drawing by Shon's 11-year-old daughter, Jocelyn Peil

merely the iceberg that caused the Titanic to sink, and it wasn't just the iceberg that killed so many people. What really caused the Titanic disaster was human arrogance. At the time, there were people who said that even God couldn't sink that ship. The truth is, the state-of-the-art design that everyone pointed to turned out to have fatal flaws that became apparent only after the disaster happened. Who would have predicted this would ever occur?

To add to the design flaw issues (and partly due to the arrogance surrounding them) the Titanic didn't carry enough lifeboats to accommodate all of the people onboard. Why should it since it was unsinkable?

The lifeboats could only accommodate 1,178 people,

but the Titanic could carry 2,435 passengers plus 900 crew members. At capacity, the ship could carry approximately 3,300 people but had lifeboats for only one-third that number.

So were there warning signs before the Titanic's fatal voyage? Yes. Were they heeded? No. And that's why the Titanic disaster is a lesson for all of us about being prepared for the worst scenarios.

There have been other disasters that have "snuck up" on us. We look back and wonder where the warnings signs were before the dot-com crash? Were there warnings before the credit crisis crash of '08? What about the COVID-19 crash in 2020? Did anyone see that one coming? Are there warning signs today? We're walking along a precipice only one step away from God only knows what happening to this country. Are we seeing the warning signs and taking the necessary precautions? Or are we living in arrogance, burying our head in the sand and hoping the disaster won't happen in our lifetime?

Roller Coasters and Lifeboats

Remember the last time you were on a roller coaster? Think about the experience. You wait in line anticipating the thrills ahead. Then you board the ride and get buckled in. Suddenly you start to move. . . click . . . click . . . click . . . You're climbing to the top, and it's all good. But when you get to the top and look down, all of a sudden, your stomach does a summersault. Your anticipation of the thrill is matched by the anxiety of the situation you've put yourself in. Maybe you close your eyes because you just don't want to look, or you take a deep breath to prepare yourself for the steep drop to come.

Here's the point: When you can see what's coming, you can prepare yourself.

On the roller coaster, you have the advantage of foresight.

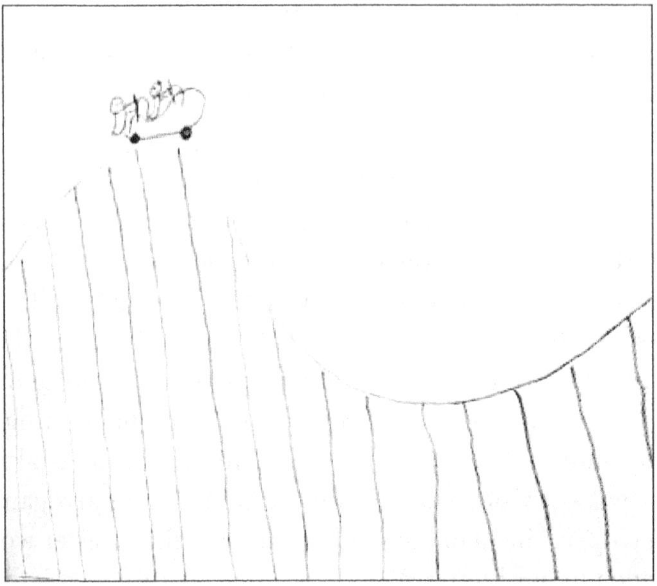

Drawing by Shon's 11-year-old son, Kolton Peil

Unfortunately, life doesn't work that way. We don't know what's coming. We can't see what's going to happen politically or with the stock market. What we do know is that when we look at the world, it's kind of a mess. And we know that at some point the market is going to correct.

That's why we always ask, "What if?" What if the government changes the rules on your investment vehicles? What if the stock market corrects before you reach safety? What if your financial ship is struck by an unseen iceberg? Have you prepared properly? Is your retirement plan set up to withstand another market correction like the ones we experienced in 2008 and 2020? Remember, it's not a matter of if but when it will happen again. Are you prepared and protected? Do you have enough financial lifeboats to save your retirement?

In our classes, we often ask for a volunteer to do a quick role play with us and say, "Okay, Mark, you're going to retire next year. Between now and then, the market is going to have a major correction. It's going to go down about 30%. How much are you comfortable losing?" And Mark says, "Nothing."

That's what everyone says, "I don't want to lose anything."

So we ask them what they have done since the last major correction to make sure they never lose money again. And again, the answer is always, "Nothing."

Our response is, "The market corrects about every seven to 10 years. We don't have time to wait. You said you want to retire in a year, so you don't have time to make up a huge loss if that happens again."

That quiets the whole room. It really gets their attention — and we hope it gets your attention. What have you put in place to make sure you don't lose any of your retirement savings in the next market correction? What is your lifeboat for when the market sinks again? We know it's going to happen . . . we just don't know when.

Retiring on Time

When John first talked with us, his money was 100% invested in the market, and he was getting nervous. He knew that he should be more conservative at his age, but he hadn't taken any action.

> He was nearing retirement, and the market was erratic. John was convinced that a market correction was soon coming. His fear of losing money caused him to look for a way to protect his money so he could retire without anxiety or concern.
>
> We listened to John's story, discussed each aspect of his plan, and created a Retirement Shield plan that fit his situation. And it's a good thing we did because, within a few weeks of creating his Retirement Shield, the market corrected significantly.
>
> Roz K.
>
> Retirement Shield Coach in Illinois

Like most people, John was taken by surprise with the rapid drop in market value. He would have lost a tremendous amount of his retirement money if his money was still in the market at that time. Fortunately, it wasn't. When the market crashed in February 2020, he didn't lose a penny. To say John was relieved and very grateful is an understatement.

The mantra when the market corrects is, "Everyone is losing money." But John knows from personal experience, that isn't true. Not everyone loses money when the market goes down.

Needless to say, John is ecstatic. He's counting down the days to his retirement at the end of this year. He's able to bank on a guaranteed retirement with his life savings protected by his Retirement Shield.

John knows that if he had not created his Retirement Shield when he did, he would have lost a significant portion of his retirement money in the crash. Instead of retiring, he would have had to work three to five more years in his current job to try to make up for his losses. Fortunately, John took action, created his Retirement Shield, and is now enjoying peace of mind and planning his first year of retirement.

Learning from History

History has a way of repeating itself. So, what have Americans learned from history? The answer is usually "nothing" because we haven't made any changes in response to the events we've lived through. And as the old saying goes, those who don't learn from history are doomed to repeat it.

Do you have a retirement plan? If you do, when did you last look at it? Has it changed at all since you first set it up? How different does it look now as compared to before? Remember, we all know it's a matter of time before the market corrects again. It's not a matter of if, but it's a matter of when.

How many times has your financial advisor reached out to you in the last couple of years to say, "Hey, let's take some winnings off the table? You're in or near retirement, and it might be time to make some changes." When was the last time your advisor reached out to you at all? This is why you want to be in a relationship that's proactive, not reactive.

Most retirement advisors are generalists, not specialists. Chances are, they're not looking at the things that can cause the next big "what if" or the next big issue within your plan — assuming that you even have a plan. As we've said before, most people don't have a plan at all.

When Gloria sat down to meet with us, she was working for the border patrol office and was planning to retire in the next year. We reviewed her plan and looked at her financials and had the unfortunate opportunity of sharing with her the reality of her situation.

Gloria called her husband to let him know that she wouldn't be retiring for a few more years because of the money that they had lost in a recent market downturn. It was heartbreaking to watch her cry while she was talking to her husband on the phone; there was so much frustration and raw emotion in her voice.

That's why we have created the Retirement Shield process and written this book. We don't want people to experience that frustration. We help our clients go through the Retirement Shield process to create a plan that protects them from the "icebergs" that could potentially come their way. This has given them the safety and freedom they want so that they can enjoy their retirement years doing what they've always dreamed of doing. The question is, does your retirement offer the same protection?

Seeing Through the Fog

From roughly 1910 to 2000, the market averaged right around 8%, but from 2000 to the crash of 2020, it has averaged only slightly better than 5.5%. Despite that fact, many financial professionals and firms would still have you believe that 8% is the average, and that's what they're building their plans around.

The market has changed foundationally, but most financial services and firms have not. What we have found with clients who have come to us for help is that they realized they could no longer expect their traditional retirement accounts to cover all they needed in retirement. Even more so, many of them lacked a plan in place to cover their lifestyle, taxes, inflation, and rising health care costs.

What happens to your money if there's another disaster in the market like in 2000, 2008, or 2020? Forget the 8% gains. You need to hope you don't lose 50% as many retirees did back then. As our clients move toward retirement, we teach them that their primary focus should be on preserving what they have. Once we've helped them identify how to protect retirement, it has allowed them to look at ways to grow the rest of their money as they see fit.

Yet advisors aren't even dealing concretely with these questions or the volatility of the market. Instead, they reassure clients by referring to any dip in the market as a paper loss. They promise that the market will always rally and that it's the greatest wealth builder there ever was. Some would say it's also the greatest wealth stealer for the uninformed.

Advisors consistently talk about growth and the rate of returns because they don't have a solution if there is no growth or return. If they keep riding the norm, you don't have time to make major changes. We all know the big banks or big money firms don't change their game plans. They're not deviating from what's made them billions of dollars over the last hundred years. They've created a way to embed fees within their portfolios, telling you to keep doing what you've been doing, all the while sitting back and collecting their lofty paychecks without making any adjustments to your accounts. They're getting wealthy whether you are or not.

The Double Loss

It's easy to get confused when advisors start talking about returns, so let's take a closer look at that. A concept that you must understand is what's called the sequence of returns. This can make all the difference to your retirement nest egg and the money you have to live on. To put it simply, the market (and your accounts) go down faster than they go up.

Most people don't realize if they have $100,000 sitting in their retirement account and the market goes down 30 percent, it takes more than a 30% increase to get back to where you started. If you take a 30% loss on $100,000, you're left with $70,000. If you regain 30% on that $70,000, you have $91,000. So you're still $9,000 short of being even. People who are retiring no longer have time on their side to wait that out.

Suppose there is a market correction three years into your retirement, how will that affect your income? Let's say you're taking out $2,000 a month, which is 5% of your account, but then the market goes down 20%. Now you have lost 20% of your nest egg, and you haven't done anything wrong. There's also nothing you can do about it. Once it's done, it's done.

The challenge is that you still need $2,000 per month. But the chances of your account ever getting to back where it was are slim to none, because now you're making withdrawals from your account instead of deposits. People forget that when they're working, they're making contributions and so the accounts bounce back faster from a loss because you're getting both market growth and your contribution.

In retirement, you're taking a distribution, which means you're taking money out of the account and you're also losing money from the market correction. So you're spending your money and the market is spending your money. It's a double loss situation.

There will be a market downturn. What happens when you're taking out income and the market goes down 30%? Now what? Are you just going to live off 30% less? Are you going to run out of money when you're 85?

What about when taxes go up? We know that's inevitable as well. If the average American family that we deal with lives on $5,000 a month and taxes go up 20%, that family is losing $1,000 a month. How are they going to replace that money? Where's it going to come from? That's the reality we all are facing.

Each one of these issues can eat away at your money. Failing to address any of these can destroy your retirement. It's no coincidence that the average age of workers at Walmart is going up. Look around the next time you go there. There are a lot of 60-somethings working because they need the money. Their pension — or lack thereof — and Social Security benefits just aren't enough. They lost money in the last downturn, need the health care benefits, or simply didn't have a plan for their retirement years.

This might sound like a lot of bad news. But through the Retirement Shield process, we've taught clients how to create a solid plan to protect their families and provide income for the rest of their lives.

The question is, what could a Retirement Shield plan look like for you? When you work with a Retirement Shield coach, they can help identify opportunities to build a custom plan with you. They're going to talk about different strategies you can put into place that can help protect your family and the money you've accumulated through the years. The beautiful thing is that you do have the ability to protect your money. You have the power to take your nest egg and make it last throughout your retirement years. You have the ability to make your money stand up against the tax code, outpace inflation, and withstand market volatility.

Diana's Sinking Ship

Diana is one of the most conservative, sweetest, and nicest people you will ever meet. She retired in 2006 with a great pension and great Social Security benefits. Diana just wanted to protect her money so she could pass it on to her family. She didn't want to be in anything risky; she's not a risky person at all. She's never even had a speeding ticket. But Diana's broker had her completely overexposed. And so when the market corrected in '08, she lost 60 percent of her nest egg.

Diana didn't even need that money to make 3% to 4% a year. She just needed it to be there and grow. It was going to fund college for the grandkids. It was going to fund family vacations. But because no one was paying attention, Diana had well over a million dollars almost completely wiped out. It was complete negligence and there was nothing she could do about it. Diana's ship was sinking.

We often see people with enough assets who don't have to take risks with their money. They don't need to double or triple their money over the next 6 to 10 years; they just need to preserve their money and let it grow. But we also consistently see people taking risks and losing assets because no one is paying attention to the "what ifs."

That's why it's so important when building a plan to ask what you want your money to do. What do you need your money to do compared to what is it currently doing?

Unfortunately, most people don't start with this simple principle, and many are taking on a lot more risk than they realize. It's why you need a second opinion, a fresh perspective on your investments and their underlying risk.

What happens if we have a terrorist attack? What happens if inflation goes up significantly? What happens if taxes go up 15% to 20%? What happens if the market loses 40% of its value? When we ask these questions, we begin to eliminate the "what ifs." We make sure you have enough lifeboats in place.

It's a cliché, but it's true: No one plans to fail, but people fail to plan. You don't know what's going to happen. We don't know what's going to happen, either. None of us have the advantage of seeing the roller coaster's next drop, so we have to build a plan that can be ready for anything. That's precisely why we created the Retirement Shield process.

In the next chapter, we'll look at what you can do to ensure your money lasts, along with some of the tools you can use to make sure you aren't gambling away your hard-earned money in the Wall Street casino.

It's impossible to hit an invisible target..

~ Shon Peil

Chapter 8

The Retirement Shield Plan

Throughout this book, we've talked about the numerous factors that can affect your retirement and threaten your financial security, which can seem like a lot of dire predictions and bad news. Now we've reached our favorite part of this discussion: detailing a process that can eliminate those scary "what ifs" and offer you confidence in your retirement years.

It's great fun for us to be able to offer a process and a plan that is simple to understand and one that gives clients a lot of confidence. We have come to realize what people really want is simplicity. They want something tangible and understandable, but they also want to feel confident and eliminate the "what ifs."

Focus on Income

What's unique about our team of Retirement Shield coaches is their ability to help address one of the top concerns of most retirees' today, and that's creating consistent income in retirement that will last a lifetime. The size of your nest egg doesn't matter nearly as much as your monthly income. As such, we focus on income, ensuring that our clients don't run out, regardless of what happens in the world. Our team of insurance and financial professionals have access to programs that are helping people all across the country who are preparing for retirement to put together an income plan that could potentially last a lifetime. Does your current plan have a lifetime income provision in place outside of Social Security?

And as Retirement Shield coaches who are focused on protecting income, we help our clients look at all of the critical areas that can affect it: Social Security, taxes, health care, hidden fees (a silent killer), and the "what if's" of the market.

We love talking about taxes. Why? Because most people aren't talking about them. Taxes have been a constant in this country for more than 100 years. They're not going to go away, and they can eat away your hard-earned money unless we do something about them. Most people expect taxes to increase eventually. Speak with a Retirement Shield coach about putting a plan in place that could reduce the impact of taxes in retirement, making your money last longer.

Health care is another area many advisors don't discuss. The Retirement Shield is one of the few processes that tackle this area head-on. Let's face it: Our country's health care system is a mess right now. Health care costs are rising and are likely to continue going up. We also know that three of four Americans will eventually have to deal with long-term care. So how do we handle all of this? Let's address it now, decide how we're going to fund it, and make it part of a comprehensive plan that identifies how we're going to take care of ourselves and our loved ones when we need to.

Downside protection is another area that any comprehensive plan needs to address. It doesn't matter how many zeros are in your portfolio; none of the advisors we work with across the country have ever met a client who was comfortable taking on more risk than they wanted or losing more money than they could easily spare.

The market is going to go up and down, but let's make sure your income isn't also going to fluctuate.¬ Who wants to ride that roller coaster of emotions? Who wants to get up every morning checking the market? Is it red? Is it green? Did I make money this quarter? Did I lose money? That's not the way to a stress-free retirement.

Most people say, "I don't want to lose any money." Well, we know the market is volatile. It fluctuates. What kind of risk are you taking right now? Do you even know what type of risk is in your existing portfolio, and are you comfortable with it? Do you understand what a major correction could do to your portfolio? You need to know how it could affect your income, spending money, travel, etc. The Retirement Shield process has helped our clients choose programs that reduce their exposure to risk while creating a protected income stream.

Hidden fees are another area that often gets overlooked. The truth is that fees are the silent killer. How do we make sure we're getting value for what we're paying (and that we're not overpaying)? Has your advisor ever explained to you the fees built into your portfolio? Based on what we hear from clients, it seems that no one can ever get a good answer to the question, "What are my fees?" The most common comment is, "Well, I asked my advisor, but I never got a straight answer." The Retirement Shield uses a "behind the curtain" approach to make sure you understand any fees that you are paying or have ever incurred, showing you how to lower those fees going forward.

We have found that most people don't understand what

their money is doing and what it should be doing. The Retirement Shield process walks you through what you want your money to be doing, what you need it to be doing, and shows you how to get it doing just that. It's a process that is different for everybody, and we tailor it to your unique situation.

We know that you don't want to lose money. We know that you don't want to pay more in fees than you have to, and you certainly don't want to pay more in taxes. Do you have a plan for all of that? You need to understand that by doing nothing, you're actually making a decision, and it's one that will leave you riding the ups and downs of that emotional roller coaster.

But the Retirement Shield is a process that creates a simple, yet comprehensive plan for all of these areas to make sure they are working together and complementing each other. This process creates an easy to follow road map for you.

Our team is here to make sure you're pulling income from the right buckets and that you are not paying any more in taxes than you are legally required to pay. We make sure you have a clear road map that removes any uncertainty from retirement. It's a comprehensive, one-stop, cover-everything approach. Once we develop a plan, it's flexible. It ebbs and flows with life because life happens. And when life happens, the plan is adjustable.

For example, let's suppose you want to take that trip to Australia in two years instead of next year. Let's adjust your plan. What if your adult child gets into a situation, and they need some financial help? Where do you get the $15,000 they need? How will you cope with having a granddaughter or grandson living with you? That's not something you planned on, and now you need an extra $1,000 a month. We'll adjust to take care of that. Not only is it essential to have a plan, but it's also important to have one that's flexible and alterable when necessary. It's not my money, and it's not my plan. It's your plan, your money, and your life.

You may be in great shape for retirement. We hope so. But if you aren't certain, why not get a second opinion? That's the opportunity you have with the Retirement Shield. You'll gain a fresh perspective to clarify what you need and want in your retirement.

After meeting with people, we often hear them say, "Oh, we should've started this 10 years ago" or, "Oh, I knew we were doing this and that. We should have done this years ago." That's okay. The most important thing is that you do something now. It's not too late.

We've all heard it all:

- "I'll never retire. I'll work till I'm 75."
- "I don't know. I just hope it's not all gone."
- "I'll just move in with my kids."
- "I just hope I don't have to rely on the state to take care of me."

What's behind all those comments is the fact that 95% of Americans have no plan for retirement and a very minimal understanding of their money. They have apprehension and fear about retirement because it's unknown. The Retirement Shield offers a way to unpack all those unknowns, eliminate the fear, and give you a plan that provides protection and peace of mind.

If you were facing major surgery, you wouldn't hesitate to get a second opinion to give you a fresh perspective so you could be sure you make the best decision. Doesn't your retirement deserve the same consideration? You certainly need to get this right. The reason you're reading the book is so that you can get it right. Knowledge is power, and this is about empowering you to take control of your retirement.

Four Simple Steps

When we sit down with people interested in the Retirement Shield process, we explain that it boils down to four simple steps:

Step One is describing just what you want in your retirement. We want to define your freedom. When you envision your retirement and the ways you want to enjoy the nest egg you've worked so hard for, what does that look like? What does retirement freedom look like to you? Is it traveling to Europe, having no debt, buying a new motor home, taking your grandkids to Disneyland? What does your ideal retirement look like?

In **Step Two**, we want to identify what would get in the way of that ideal retirement. What might threaten it? Remember, knowledge is power. Identifying all the current threats that could eat away your money will allow you to stop these things in their tracks. Because if we don't start to remove those obstacles, you're going to have to start eliminating things from your bucket list. You're not going to be able to do the things you always wanted to do.

Step Three examines your portfolio to free up any hidden income and find ways to make your money last longer, such as choosing the right time to take Social Security and reducing taxes on your retirement account. It's all about understanding how to maximize your money because every dollar matters. You worked hard for them, and they belong to you.

Then, in **Step Four**, we produce a comprehensive plan that considers your wants and aspirations in retirement while providing stability and protection. A Retirement Shield process can help guarantee the money that is set aside for retirement will last.

Those are our four steps. Step five is up to you. That's where you get to imagine buying that RV or taking that cross-country trip you've always dreamed of and not having a single care in the world. Imagine not having to worry about what the market is doing or whether someone's going to sign a new bill into law cutting your money in half. Imagine taking all your grandchildren to Disneyland and making lifelong memories. Ultimately, your Retirement Shield plan will allow you to use your money to create the memories you've dreamed about for years. Your money becomes a tool that will empower you to make your own financial decisions and allow you to have freedom in retirement and an income that you can never outlive.

Two Obvious Choices

At this point you have two choices: One is to stay on the path that you're currently on, cross your fingers, and hope taxes never go up, the market never corrects, and that you never have to move into a long-term care facility. You can ride the emotional roller coaster of looking at your accounts every day, wondering if you'll lose it all and what that will cost you. Take the chance of outliving your money and calling your kids to see if they have a spare room.

OR …

You can be proactive. Get ahead of the challenges that are coming by getting help from an experienced professional who is a specialist in retirement income planning and protection.

Approximately 9 out of 10 clients we meet will end up running out of money in their early 80s if they keep doing what they're doing. But every professional they've worked with has led them to believe they have plenty of money and everything's going to be fine. How can that be? It's because those professionals are using the old tools. They plan as though the market is always going to return between 8% and 10%. They plan as though taxes are always going to stay low. They plan as though inflation will never go up beyond 2%. The truth is that none of the tools currently being used to address most people's retirement plans are adequate. It often seems that they plan for the best-case scenario and never consider the worst-case scenario. That's just not realistic.

No Surprises

Surprises can be fun, but not when it comes to your retirement. Just ask Jerry and Janet. They had a retirement plan and believed that they had enough for their future and that everything was going to be great. But they never considered the impact of taxes and a market downturn. As long as taxes never went up and the market never went negative, they were fine. But they were shocked to learn that if the market had any volatility whatsoever and taxes went up a little bit, they would run out of money at ages 82 and 83.

Another thing that they hadn't looked at was Jerry's pension. If Jerry died, how much of his pension would Janet get? We discovered that she wouldn't get 75% or even 50% and had to share with them that she wouldn't receive anything.

Jerry's entire pension would be gone once he passed away. To say they were surprised was an understatement.

Jerry and Janet thought everything was fine, but they weren't working with real numbers. No one had ever taken the time to sit down with them and look at what could happen.

- What would happen if the market didn't always return 8%?
- What would happen if Jerry died before Janet?

No one had taken the time in the last 15 years to figure out how much of the pension she would get. The reality was that unless they did something differently, there would be significant consequences. Janet would not have enough money if Bob died, and they were going to run out of money if they both lived. They had never imagined that this was even a possibility. We were able to reallocate their assets and establish an income plan for them. Now they can live the rest of their lives without having a shortfall of money, and Janet is protected should Jerry pass away. They are both much happier knowing they are protected and safe for the rest of their lives.

You have to be proactive. You owe it to yourself to get a second opinion. The problem with being reactive is that once the damage is done, it's done. You can't go back and replace lost money. You can't go back and lower your tax burden. The time to act is now.

It's Never Too Late

Even if you are already retired, it's not too late to adjust your retirement plan. Recently, we met with Phil (82) and

Patricia (70). They have been retired for years and have about $300,000 in investible assets, and they wondered how their accounts were performing.

When we asked them how they were doing for income and whether they felt they had everything in place, both said everything was fine. They talked about how great Phil's pension is, so we asked how much of it Patricia would receive if George died. Patricia said she would get about 30% of it, which meant she would be losing about $1,000 a month.

Phil spoke up and said, "Yeah, but she's going to get my Social Security." They didn't realize that she would get Phil's $2,000 Social Security check, but she would lose her own $1,000 in Social Security.

If Phil passes away, Patricia loses $2,000 a month. They had never talked about that or thought it through. So we worked with them to put a plan in place that would take care of Patricia. Now her money is set up to grow and be there so that it will cover the income gap and replace the income that she will lose if Phil dies first. There's a very good chance, given their age difference, that Patricia will outlive Phil. But no one had ever brought that up. Now that they have a Retirement Shield in place, they are protected and have great peace of mind.

Protecting Your Family

Remember, you and your spouse are not the only ones affected by your retirement plan or the lack thereof. The ripple effect can reach your kids and grandkids, something Michael and Mary realized when they came to us for help with planning and insurance issues. Both were in their early 60s. Michael was a retired factory worker who was receiving a life-only pension. There was no survivor benefit to pass to Mary, which meant they had nothing in place to protect their family if anything happened to Michael. Mary's exact words were, "I'd be up a creek if he dies."

They needed a plan. Michael and Mary had about $100,000 left on their mortgage, and downsizing wasn't an option with their grandkids living three blocks away. If anything ever happened to Michael, they wanted to know that Mary would be protected so that she could stay in their home, have enough income, and take care of the grandkids. So we created a plan that accomplished their desires. Nine months later, Michael died of a yeast infection. Who could have seen that coming? But because we had a plan, Mary was protected. She was able to provide the care their grandkids needed and has the income she needs for the rest of her life.

These are all real-life stories and just a few examples of how the Retirement Shield protects individuals and families.

The future is predictable: Change is coming. But you don't have to be a victim of it. Act now, create a plan for your family, and know that you are prepared for whatever circumstances the future holds.

We'd love the opportunity to help you create a Retirement Shield plan for your family. Together we'll look at what you desire in retirement, the major threats you'll face, and discuss the best way to establish an income plan that's right for you.

A Retirement Shield coach can help you put all the pieces in place to complement each other. You've worked all your life to earn your money; it's time to make your money work for you.

Conclusion

Thank you for reading this book. We hope we have given you some things to think about and convinced you that you don't need to fear the word retirement. Your life doesn't have to stop when your paycheck does.

Our goal has been to shine some light on the five major areas you need to consider when it comes to retirement, showing you that you can gain control over those areas and your retirement.

The Retirement Shield process and plan give you that control. By considering income, taxes, health care, fees, and risk management, you can create the retirement you've always wanted. You can have an income plan that manages your distribution and maximizes your Social Security. You can minimize your tax burden. You can minimize your fees, manage your risks, and protect your assets from market volatility. And you can have peace of mind in your retirement. Reach out to the person who handed you this book and schedule a time to meet. In a 15- or 20-minute meeting, they can offer you a second opinion and a fresh perspective on your particular retirement concerns. Ultimately, it's all about making sure your money is doing what you want it to do and, more importantly, what you need it to.

Let's talk.

About the Authors

Shon Peil has spent the past 20 years in the retirement planning industry, where he takes great joy in helping clients protect their retirement assets while building their financial legacies for future generations.

He started his career working with other retirement professionals around the country, teaching them how they could help their clients optimize their Social Security benefits and retirement income. Today, Shon works with Retirement Plus clients to build relationships and work toward financial independence. He is also a National Coach for the Retirement Shield program.

Shon finds his most rewarding role and true purpose in life is that of being a husband and a father. He and his wife Hillary have three sons and two daughters. Outside of the office, he enjoys following college football, coaching his kids' teams, and spending summer days at the family's lake cabin.

Roz Kovel is the founder and president of X-It Strategies, Inc. She is a preeminent retirement expert who has been helping clients avoid risk and prepare for retirement since 2002. Roz is passionate about providing financial education to the people she serves. Because of her own previous lack of knowledge and information about finances, she experienced tremendous losses when personal and investment crises happened. As a result, she is committed to making sure her clients have all the information they need to make informed decisions about their money.

Roz holds a Bachelor of Arts in psychology from the University of Illinois/Champaign and a Master of Arts in behavior modification from the University of Kansas. When she is not working, Roz loves seeing movies on the big screen. She's also an avid reader and enjoys spending time with her grandchildren and learning about that generation's interests (video games and YouTube!). Roz is also in the process of training her 3-year-old golden retriever, Spencer, to become a therapy dog.

You can contact Roz at:
X-It Strategies, Inc.
2625 Butterfield Road
Suite 138S
Oak Brook, IL 60523
Website: https://www.x-itstrategies.com/
Email: rkovel@x-itstrategies.com
Phone: (630) 852-8900

Expert Press

www.ExpertPress.net

Made in the USA
Monee, IL
19 October 2026

66036210R00069